INFORMATION TECHNOLOGY IN 21ST CENTURY

INFORMATION TECHNOLOGY IN 21ST CENTURY

(In 9 Volumes)

UNIVERSAL ACCESS TO INFORMATION RESOURCES

(Volume 1)

PROF. RAMESH CHANDRA

Vice-Chancellor, Bundelkhand University, Jhansi (U.P.)

Publication

KALPAZ PUBLICATIONS

DELHI–110052

INFORMATION TECHNOLOGY IN 21ST CENTURY
Universal Access to Information Resources
(Information Technolgy)

Rs. 8000 (Set)
Rs. 900 (each volume)

ISBN: 81-7835-158-7 (Set)
ISBN: 81-7835-159-5 (Vol. 1)

Published in 2003 in India by
Kalpaz Publications
C-30, Satyawati Nagar
Delhi-110052
E-mail: kalpaz@hotmail.com

Laser Typesetting at: A.S. Printers
Printed at: Chawla Offset Printers, Delhi

Preface

The internet represents a new collective mental space. With the advent of the internet, nations, regions, cities, villages, and individuals are able to work and to come together within global, networked communities based on shared interests at a speed and inclusiveness never before possible. It is critical to ensure that all societies gain the opportunity to merge their existing worlds into, and become a part of an expanded world—that includes the new virtual world. Leaving the creation of this newly expanded world of ours to technocrats, engineers and the sway of multinationals is a recipe for a world that we would not want to bequeath to future generations.

It is important to understand that lowering the barriers to internet access is helpful to everyone in the context of gaining easier access to information. An argument can be made that every individual should have the right to access information—regardless of disability, economic situation, or geographic location. Without this realization there will be no consistent progress in the effort to provide global access. Cost of access has to come down to where not just the elite in emerging nations can afford to get on the internet.

Access to the internet without the ability to use the content is a hollow shell. Access to the Internet without the ability to use the features or participate in e-commerce is nothing more than lip service to the idea of universal access. The benefits of addressing the problems of inaccessible design extend to include all people, including the community of people with disabilities. There must not be even more of a digital divide opened between people with disabilities and the efforts to provide internet access to all in emerging economies.

UNESCO and other non-governmental organisations can play a vital communications role in helping to educate and galvanize governments and the public at large to understand how fundamentally important it is to put into place a free public communications framework. One that is non discriminatory to all voices, commercial and non-commercial; and that ensures that adequate space on the network, regardless of technology, is reserved for undistorted— substantive forms of information, dialogue and debate. Universal access to the Internet will then be able to happen and to flourish through one critical mediating institution: namely, the institutional infrastructure of public space.

This book will prove highly informative to administrators, policy planners, teachers, researchers and students in the field of information technology.

Editor

Contents

PROF. A.R. KIDWAI, Ph.D. (Cornell, USA)
Member of Parliament (Rajya Sabha)
Formerly: Chairman, UPSC & Governor of
Bihar and West Bengal

सत्यमेव जयते

FOREWORD

Human civilisation advanced through various stages, from the Stone Age to the period of industrial revolution, as a gradual process. With the increasing scientific knowledge of Nature and its forces man's ability to harness natural resources to his advantage has increased by leaps and bounds. The second half of the twentieth century was marked by the developments of atomic energy, space and electronics which accelerated human progress with phenomenal speed. Thus, the development of Information Technology, which is the result of man's conquest of space and electronics, has revolutionalised means of communication irrespective of physical distance and has changed the concept of time and space. Today, the application of Information Technology has influenced all aspects of human life including business and banking, social and political interaction, scientific and cultural activities. Therefore, people have to adapt themselves to the new mode and style of living in the age of Information Technology and Cyberspace to keep pace with the emerging new global society.

In nine volumes, the author Prof. Ramesh Chandra has weaved the theme on "Information Technology in 21st Century" in a fairly comprehensive and comprehensible style focussing on several aspects of information highways, free software, the role of global information society, access to information sources, searching on the web, information as a global asset, responsibilities of information systems, multilinguism in Cyberspace, rural accessibility, management information system and financial sectors including business and banking, governance through internet, digital divide, UNESCO as a forum, freedom in Cyberspace, information systems accountability, cybercensorship, impact on social, political and economic activities. The additional academic information has been meticulously provided at the end of each volume. It is the well-chosen and standard works of eminent writers whose writings could fill up the relevant gaps at various levels. The Appendices too are fairly meaningful and enhance the prestige of these volumes.

The exhaustive work of Prof. Ramesh Chandra will be very useful for researchers, teachers and students while assessing the scientific progress in the field of Information Technology. I was, indeed, very happy to go through the numerous details given in these nine volumes. The problems and concepts have been explained in simple terms for the benefit of technical as well as non-technical persons. Today, Information Technology is an important professional tool for scientists, engineers, teachers and students, writers, journalists and businessmen who can make full use of these volumes as readily available source.

I know we have to traverse a long way on the difficult terrains, particularly in this burgeoning area of science, romantically known as Information Technology. But I am confident that with dedicated efforts in this field we shall be able to attain international standards in communications, commerce and industry and have access to the expanding areas of knowledge at our fingertips.

October 19, 2002

(A.R. Kidwai)

1

Introduction

Electronic information markets have become one of the major topics of discussion in international business and also in information science. This chapter presents the information point of view. What will be the contribution of these new markets to the production, distribution, and use of knowledge? Will information markets support the transformation of already produced knowledge into information that can be used in actual problem situations? And what does that mean for the balance of knowledge between developing and developed countries? Are electronic markets a means of overcoming the knowledge gap or will they rather deepen it?

Information is increasingly considered as the main factor for innovation in all fields in all countries in the world. This is not only true for high-technology countries but also, in particular, for developing countries which struggle to overcome the gap between rich and poor. 'Rich and poor' is nowadays reformulated as 'information rich and information poor'. To have or not to have access to information is the basis for all progress in science, economy, culture, and society as a whole. Traditionally, libraries, archives, and publishing companies with knowledge products in print form have been responsible for the provision of knowledge as a source for information. In the last twenty years, electronic online data bases have taken advantage of the new telecommunication networks and computer facilities and have provided additional and increasingly important information products and information services. These electronic services have constituted the information electronic market or, to put it in terms of a macro-economic concept, have founded the information economy, which can be considered as the growing, if not dominant sector of contemporary economies, at least in highly developed countries.

At present, again with the advent of international networks (the Internet), new online services have arisen on the market. These so called value-added services are in general end-user friendly systems due to the application of hypertext methodology and the use of the WWW software. These new online systems have changed electronic/information markets dramatically in the last 5 years. Information markets are no longer domain-specific markets which are managed by information specialists only. They are public information markets, which means that they are not only publicly available but also accessible and usable by in principle everybody. They can be directly distributed world-wide without any further organizational support.

Easy production, easy distribution, and easy access and usage—this leads many people to believe that a brave new information world will soon be within the reach where everybody from everywhere can profit from these new information products. There is little doubt that new information and communication technologies and services have the potential for constructing a new world order. But this is not an automatic process. International organizations such as UNESCO must play an active part in structuring it.

In contrast to the optimistic view - everything in the information world is becoming easier and better, due to advanced technology - we would like to emphasize that so far only highly developed countries have profited from the development of electronic information markets. They profit in a twofold way: 'On the one hand they have access to information resources because the international networks are at their disposal and they have the appropriate information technology infrastructure. They are the effective users of information. They use information as the basis for continuing innovation in all fields of the economy. On the other hand they have the knowledge and the market power to buy data from everywhere, to produce and distribute information that will increasingly be bought by information customers on a world-wide basis. They are the producers and sellers of information and thus constitute a new economy, the information or knowledge industry.

Being an information rich country therefore no longer means only the right of access to information but also the chance to produce, distribute and sell information. The ability to 'read' information is no longer sufficient. The right to information and communication is also the right to 'write' information. In advanced societies information products are the main source for the GNP and the majority of the employed find their work place in the information economy. Although this is so far more a characteristic feature of high technology countries, in the future it will be of relevance for all countries in the world. Is this process of informatization mainly a process of transferring experience from the advanced world to the developing world? Or is their a chance for these nations to find their own path towards the information society?

In the last thirty years the discussion about the best way of supporting developing countries has often been a discussion about appropriate technology: What is an appropriate technology for a developing country taking in account the specific circumstances of the country such as state of technology and education, primary needs, country-typical potentials, etc. It does not make any sense to import technical systems which have been developed and have proved to be useful in a high-technology environment to a different context. And the same may be true today with the import of information and the usage of information market products. What is appropriate information? And who decides which information needs to be produced by whom? And what are the organizational/institutional means for building appropriate information devices? This will lead us to the idea of regional electronic market places based on regional information competence.

The international information markets (users and producers) are at the moment heavily dominated by the western world, in particular by US-American interests or the interests of the so-called G7/8-nations. This is true not only for network development but also for information market places and information services. International players such as Knight-Ridder, Lexis/Nexis, Mead, Reuters, Reed, FT Profile, CAS (Chemical Abstract

Services), Engineering Information, M.A.I.D. (Market Analysis and Information Database) - to mention only a few - dominate the (old) international online data base markets and the same is true for the new online services, the so-called value-added services such as CompuServe, AOL (American Online), Microsoft Network Services, etc. These services collect information, produce services and sell them.

They dominate the information markets and have a monopoly on defining the content of the service. Information about a national market, let us say about Poland, is easier to retrieve from these international sources than from some national information infrastructure.

Most of the countries in the world deliver only the raw material, the data, and are forced to rebuy the final information product from the international content providers, the online value-added services. This situation in the information age is comparable to the flow of raw material (at low cost) and final products (at high cost) between countries at different stages of development in the industrial age.

The advent of new information and communication technology provides an opportunity for new participants to enter information markets at low investment costs. And we consider (appropriate) new regional electronic market places as an ideal means for developing countries to establish their own information culture and thus to become active members of the global information market and the global information society.

To make these general ideas somewhat clearer we'd like to proceed in the following way: First, we shall explain the concept of electronic market place as the organizational or institutional realization of the principles of electronic market. Then we shall concentrate on regional market places and work out their potential for building a new economic and cultural identity. Finally, we shall apply the idea of a regional market place to the situation of developing or under-privileged countries, and give some proposals on how to realize these market places.

One might argue that there is no need to structure the new world-wide online information scene. There is one global market and everyone can contribute to this market by writing their information on the open Internet sky. And as a matter of fact, there are many million web sites (WWW applications) available. At the moment (early 1997) a new Web site is being opened every three minutes. But this information richness - as impressive as it is - produces new problems, mainly caused by the complexity of the information market.

Although there are already powerful search engines for Web sites and other information services, orientation is becoming a major problem for end-users. This orientation problem is even greater than it was on the traditional online-market with its 7000 online databases. In this situation it turns out that for orientation purposes it is helpful, if not necessary, for information services to be bundled according to systematic or geographical criteria. An appropriate bundle constitutes an information market place.

Information market places can thus be considered organizational or institutional platforms for the information economy. They structure the general market. Information market places can be organized according to content (examples are market places for touristic purposes, for the field of engineering, for an academic discipline such archaeology) or geographical extent: there are city, regional, national or global market places on the market. A regional market place in Wroclav contains all kinds of information about Wroclac and structures information for the people living there. It also opens this regional market place to the rest of the world because regional markets places are in an international network connected to the global market.

Let us briefly give some basic information about information markets and their technological background. We have coined the new concept of telemediatics in order to emphasize the close interrelation between telecommunications, informatics (computer science) and multi-hypermedia. Information market products are based on telemediatics. It is the combination of these two, formerly separate fields, online and hypermedia, which has produced the current breakthrough of online service as a source of information for the public.

The breakthrough is within the reach of everyone although at the time being, it is still a minority of the population that has access to the telecommunication networks and information market products and services. In countries such as Germany the percentage of the population that has access to online networks is still under 10% and the percentage of people who use information services actively and continuously is still under 2% of the population. This is partly due to the negative influence of the Post/Telekom monopoly in combination with a high price policy for network usage which is prohibitive for many private customers. In the English-speaking world and in the countries of northern Europe the active usage rate is much higher, while the usage in many developing countries is still unacceptably low, without no realistic perspective for overcoming this barrier in the near future. This is one of the major challenges for international organizations such as UNESCO, namely to provide these countries with access to networks as a basis for using value-added-services and for building their own services. Access to these networks is the basis or condition for active usage and participation and not a purpose in itself. Internet access rate is an important indicator, but what really counts is the degree of active participation both in the use and production of information.

We have already mentioned the two worlds of online service—the old online data bases and the new value-added services (in the Internet but also in other proprietary online services). To make the market situation somewhat more transparent we can distinguish the following stages or types of electronic market which will be realized as concrete electronic market places. These can be interpreted as stages in the historical development but also as systematic distinctions which still coexist:

?domain-specific information markets - production of knowledge in science and technology with users in professional environments 'markets for business-to-business - organizations in business and administration with professional users in business and administration' markets for public administration - public administration organizations with users in public administration organizations 'markets for the public - organizations in business and administration with individual private users' private individual markets - individual private users who communicate with other individual private users As already mentioned, electronic markets realize market mechanisms with the support of telemediatics (telecommunication, computer science and multi/ hypermedia). With respect to commerce we distinguish between electronic shopping and business-to-business.

Electronic Shopping

Material economic goods or their substitutes (goods in their material form cannot be really transported on electronic markets, only their electronic substitutes) are the objects of trade on electronic markets. The real advantage of electronic markets becomes obvious with immaterial (information) goods, which may stem from commerce, but, as will be shown below, also from public administration, politics, science and the social or cultural world. Electronic markets support all processes of presentation, marketing, information, communication and transaction.

On electronic markets information objects are available without any limitation of time or space. This furthers the process of what is now called the virtualization of markets and business relations. Users of electronic market places can easily access a large number of offers from different competitors at any time and from any place. Electronic goods (products and services) are increasingly being demanded for and used by private end-users on electronic markets for the public. Information/content providers are reaching more and more customers via electronic market places cost-effectively and flexibly with easily up-datable product information. The technical barriers for content providers are becoming lower and lower. Intermediaries have new opportunities to make electronic market places accessible to providers and to offer integrated problem solutions for end-users. Traditional intermediaries - in particular with respect to consumer markets - are increasingly being replaced by end-user-oriented services.

Business-to-business

Electronic markets also support all kinds of business-to-business transactions. They supply information leading upto a possible commercial transaction. They help in the search for potential business partners and in providing information about market trends. They enable providers to develop attractive products and thus stimulate demand. They help to carry out all kinds of commercial transactions, e.g. transportation, insurance, customs payment financing logistics.

The main advantage of commercial electronic market places - besides the new potential for marketing - lies in lowering all kinds of transaction costs. This allows producers to attract new customers and customers to buy products at a lower prices. The (often windfall) profits from the decrease in transaction costs is the main reason for producers to participate actively in information market places and is also the main basis, together with new income from advertisement, for the providers of electronic market places.

The potential of electronic market places can be summarized as follows:

— presenting the organization in total, thus building corporate identity and image 'presenting products and services in a flexible, adaptable and easy-to-update way' maintaining active contact with current customers and winning new customers 'allowing tailored marketing (in principle 1-to-1-marketing)' making competitive positioning easier 'building strategic alliances' establishing new cooperative relations with (virtual) business partners 'supporting all kinds of transactions, such as electronic payment' providing background information about all business processes

Electronic of information markets are without doubt a challenge for the economy. But they will also influence the lives of all social groups and public organizations (administration/politics) and are to this extent a public task as well. Electronic markets therefore have a non-commercial information function which is of public interest. In the future they will allow citizens to participate actively in all aspects of their lives be it commerce, culture, education, science, politics, administration, or leisure. Information market places are thus a means of furthering public information and communication.

Advanced societies will be measured not only by the degree to which they make electronic shopping and business-to-business relations possible, but, also, by the extent to which they allow their citizens to structure their lives on an information basis, to the extent they provide access to the information they want and need. Information, without doubt, is becoming more and more a free good to be negotiated and exchanged on the market. But information is additionally a public good, which must be treated and organized carefully from a public point of view.

In the past, the main focus of attention has been on global electronic market places. Online information services such as AOL, CompuServe or MSN are the global players in the new information economy.

Despite the advent of global information systems and markets, regional or sometimes even local electronic market places are an ideal means of organizing information and communication and of serving end-users´ needs.

We consider regional market places as an important vehicle in the process of building new economic power and social/cultural/political awareness/identity. Regional electronic market places—this is the main assumption—enhance the economy and public information as well.

To support this assumption we use our experience with setting up and running the Electronic Mall Bodensee (for the lake of Constance), an example of an international regional market place covering those parts of Germany, Austria and Switzerland which border on the lake of Constance.

The Electronic Mall Bodensee is one of the biggest regional electronic market places in the German-speaking world and can therefore serve as an empirical basis for the concept of regional market places.

In the past, the regional economy has been highly influenced by the way in which the physical transport of goods could be organized. These classical positioning factors - the degree of access to the railway, highway/ interstate or shipping systems—must be reevaluated with the event of information and communication technologies. Today, physical traffic will of course not be totally replaced but electronic traffic plays an increasingly important role.

How electronic traffic is regionally organized (by electronic regional market places) is much more under the control of the region than it was with the physical circumstances of traditional markets. Regional market places can compensate for existing commercial deficits in particular in rural, cross-border areas and in all regions of the world which have not been able to play an active role in the global economy so far. The existence of a well functioning regional electronic market places can therefore be an essential competitive factor influencing the future of the region, the regional economy and social life as a whole.

What are the main features of regional market places:

— They provide a platform for all business and public information and communication activities; they allow electronic shopping for all who wish to do so; they further regional business-to-business relations, and they build up new relations between public administration and the citizens. 'Regional market places are part of the global network of market places.' Regional market places embed the cities and villages in the region by allowing them to (re)define their own local and as part of a region on an electronic basis.

They are not a new form of provincialism. Instead they allow people to organize their lives according to regionally specific circumstances. Among these regional factors is of course the local language. In regional markets places the local language of the people who live there can be used. Global market places tend to be dominated by the English language, but this will not be accepted as the day-to-day-language of communication in many non-English speaking countries. Those aspects of information which are of word-wide interest may be presented in the local language and in English. 'Regional market places provide devices by which world-wide information can be accessed from a regional point of view. They should, as a minimum, provide links to other regional market places and information services, and, as a special service, provide intelligent agents which are able to select regionally specific information from external resources.

— Regional market places should provide regional-specific information which is more or less stable and time-independent, e.g. from culture, history, science. This information can be used by the regional population but is also open to interested parties, in principle all over the world. The regional market places can become a marketing instrument for the region both in terms of economy and culture, tourism, etc. In addition regional market places provide all kinds of dynamic information which is of more local/regional interest, such as weather forecast; opening hours for movies, theatres, exhibitions; traffic, local sport information, etc.

— The value of regional market places will be defined by the extent to which they allow interactive participation. Market places are not only a new form of distribution and selling but also a means for active information behaviour. 'Regional market places further communication between the citizens of the region and should thus provide communication boards at all levels of society, simple chat boards, domain-specific mastered discussion groups, forums for political exchange when elections take place.' Regional market places, like all electronic market places, are a means of orientation and should thus provide rich metainformation & orientation tools, such as search engines, guided tours, classification schemata, and interactive help desks. 'There is no need for a single market place, instead, the regional market place should be organized as a common platform where numerous regional content providers can be bundled. A regional market place should be open for all providers from business, administration and all other groups of society.' There are many ways of organizing regional market places. It turns out that the most effective way of organizing an electronic regional market place (as a platform for all electronic regional market activities) is to avoid a monopoly, be it from public providers (public administration), from the media (a dominant newspaper), from business (a dominant regional enterprise or the chamber of commerce and trade) or from a scientific organization (a university in the region).

There is no general solution to this problem, but the main regional actors should be incorporated in the operative responsibility of the market place. ?Additionally, there are many ways of financing regional market places. Initially, there may be some public support, justified by the advantage expected for the whole region. Regional markets, being a part of the market as a whole, should be economically managed, at least in the long perspective. Regional advertisement will be the main financial basis; traditional regional media should therefore be embedded in one way or the another in the management of the market place.

As we have already mentioned, there are many ways of defining an electronic market place. Among these is geography. Nothing seems more obvious than to define a region by its geographical location. But is this still true at a time when the majority of markets factors - and region is such a factor as well - are being redefined according to the conditions of information and communication technology? Do electronic market places still mirror geographical conditions? The main characteristic of electronic market places in general is communication independent of time and space.

Time-independent, asynchronous communication is the main factor in global markets along with space-independent presentation and buying of products. Telecommunication does not care about border restrictions. And therefore we argue that the extension of a regional market place cannot be exclusively determined by physical space and borders but should be redefined by the degree of communication, on an electronic basis. We propose to define regional market places in terms of the interconnectedness of the actors coming together on this market place.

Communication processes between persons and organizations create highly interconnected virtual spaces. The degree of interconnectedness in virtual spaces can be measured in terms of the number of relations between heterogeneous actors. Intensive relations constitute a market place. If, for example, there are many contacts between people and organizations in Constance, Graz and Edinburgh; then this communicative network constitutes a new region. In practice, however, the likelihood of creating completely new regions under the influence of communication technology is not extremely high. Our hypothesis is that high connectivity in virtual spaces corresponds to high connectivity in geographic space. Of course, it is in principle possible for a regional economy to rely on the technological knowledge of a very remote university, but in reality technology transfer is easier to manage with the local university. Physical goods can be transported from all over the world but it is more likely that they will be bought within the close neighborhood. The service in a regional hospital is more likely to be used than the service from a very remote hospital. People and organizations are not isolated, context-free atoms in global networks, but are determined by real communicative relations to other people and other organizations.

The historical, political, social, cultural, and linguistic background is a useful basis for the development of stable regional networks and market places in global networks. Connectivity in these new market places becomes weaker at the borders of networks. Subnets may belong to different regional markets. Regional markets thus overlap and are embedded in national and global market places.

By advocating the concept of virtual regions we are not suggesting that the concept of traditionally defined regions be abandoned. On the contrary, new electronic regional market places are a good way to improve regional identity. The process of centralization in economy and politics as well (for example in Europe) is not reversible but can be made more acceptable by improving the regional and local situation. This is the Lebenswelt where people live and communicate with each other. On the other hand, new electronic market places as virtual regions can overcome restrictions which have been created by political decisions of the past. This means a new opportunity for regions in those parts of the world, such as in Africa, where traditional regional and cultural bonds have been dissolved by 19th-century colonialism.

Electronic market places are forms for realizing time- and space-independent principles of the electronic market in general. Market places are narrowly defined as information and communication places. Regional electronic market places are defined by the extent of interconnectivity between the actors in the region. Virtuality is primarily measured via communicative behaviour. Regional electronic markets organize the free flow of information in a twofold sense: They help in the access of information from all over the world and they support the competence of regional experts in organizing their own information, for use in their commercial and public businesses and accessible on demand for the rest of the world.

Regional electronic market places encourage information and communication autonomy both in developing and developed countries. Due to its low entrance barriers, the market place technology can develop into prime information technology for developing countries and thereby become a means of narrowing the gap between the information rich and the information poor. It is the responsibility of international organizations of supporting developing countries in constructing and running their own regional market places. But also other regions in the world should be encouraged to invest in these regional market places as a counter-model to the information hegemony of global information players.

2

Information Highways

The information highways, the population may be divided in three groups: (i) those who do not understand yet what the information highways are and how they can be used; (ii) those who already understand them; (iii) those who already understand what they are not and how they should not be used.

The author sees the information highways as a tool for a multipersonal game whose players have their own particular goals but may not be conscious of the goals of other participants. Hence, the ethics of using information highways can be considered as a set of general rules imposed on it for a common interest. He warns that the absence of such commonly accepted rules will lead to a state of informational anarchy.

The free right to express independent opinions, to do research, obtain and spread information and opinions without any restrictions and by all means, has been stated as one of the basic rights in the Universal Declaration of Human Rights of the United Nations Organization.

The further development of the right for information can be found in art. 27 of the Declaration, stating the human right to use the achievements of art and science and to protect moral and material advantages resulting from any human activity in the field of science, literature or art.

It has been stated though (art. 29 of the Declaration), that every human being, in spite of his rights and freedom, undergoes certain restrictions imposed by law, and resulting from the necessity to protect the same rights and freedoms for all people, moral norms, requirements of public order, and welfare of the democratic society.

When the Universal Declaration of Human Rights was proclaimed, nobody expected such a rapid development of computer era (there were only a few computers of the first generation existing). In many countries public television has not been known yet, mass communication media were only press and radio, and individual communication media were: telephone, telegraph, and mail. In spite of that, both the basic, affirmative, and the final, restrictive, parts of the Declaration have not, for the 50 years, become outdated.

Still, the further years have shown that the range of the accepted restrictions imposed on the commonly accepted general human right for information according to the legal systems of particular countries can be interpreted in various ways. As time passed, the differences in interpretation of the right for information between the countries of different political systems and different levels of social and economic development were increasing.

It became clear at the beginning of the seventies, when the project of UNESCO Declaration was discussed, concerning the regulations of using satellite broadcasts (the Declaration was approved during the XVII Session of the UNESCO General Conference in 1972). The communist countries, as well as many countries of the Third World, were not going to stop restricting free information flow by technical and legal means.

Although the arguments about protection of moral values and personal properties of the individuals were used, it was clear that the core of the argument was concerning free distribution of political information. It should not be assumed, though, that legal regulations restricting access to information can completely stop the flow of information. It only means that in some countries, including Poland, in certain historical periods, a very high price had to be paid for the access to information. That is why nowadays, when democratic rules of political life have returned, the society so reluctantly accepts the necessity of restricting the access to information or controlling it for the sake of some superior goals.

The societies are able to understand and accept the need of introducing ethical and legal norms which do not allow for violating personal properties (including intellectual values or economic interest) through unlimited flow of information, but they are against the unlimited control of the state over establishing such norms. Any slogans which suggest introducing, in more or less hidden form, of the moral preventive censorship in press and other publications, are highly unpopular. But it does not mean society is favourable to pornography. It rather means the society would like to participate in deciding what is permitted, and what is forbidden in its own interest. Poland is one of those countries which began to apply computer technology relatively early. Research started at the beginning of the fifties, and by the end of the fifties several original constructions of the first generation computers were already existing. By the end of the sixties trade versions of the second generation computers were applied in economy, science, and didactics.

At the beginning of the seventies attempts were made to elaborate a long-term programme of computerization of economy and state administration. For the first time the concepts of computer network based on countrywide network of data transmission ("information highway") appeared. They aimed at improving the centralized system of managing economy, and as such have originally met the approval of the authorities. But the concepts disregarded technical and economic limitations, at thus the programme of their realization was considerably restricted.

Studies over the systems which were to be constructed at that time have shown the range and significance of the legal problems which appear in connection with building systems of central planning, electronic census, state statistics, scientific and technical information, etc. At that time the state had not only the monopoly in deciding about import, production, and distribution of computers, or about development of telecommunication network in the country, but also, as the programme of information systems development started, in deciding on kind of information stored and processed by the central and local systems, on the suppliers of the information, its users, etc. In some circles the first moral and legal doubts have appeared concerning the unlimited right of the state to store personal information about its citizens, the compliance of the scientific and technical information systems with the copyright law, etc. Still, there was no escape from the informatics era. After the first stage of development, in which only very few people knew what the computers were and what their possible applications could be, the society entered the next stage, in which the knowledge about where and how computers and computer networks can be used became common.

This common knowledge about computers is due, to a high degree, to introducing computer science at secondary schools and universities. Poland's experience shows that the popularization of computer science is one of the prerequisites for common access to information, as it is understood by the Universal Declaration of Human Rights. This commonness, though, requires not only the common knowledge on computers, but also the common access to computers or terminals. The real progress in this field has occurred in Poland only in the last few years, and has been connected with social and economic changes which resulted in market economy development. In that time both computer hardware and software markets have rapidly developed.

The recent years are also the period of multimedia databases market quick expansion. It is very advantageous that the majority of buyers are university and secondary students. The programme of countrywide computer network (NASK - Scientific Academic Computer Network) covering all the major academic centres has been realized for the last few years. NASK subscribers are also connected to Internet. The estimated number of Internet subscribers in Poland is about 500

000. At the same time general purpose networks - metropolitan range (MAN) are built, and many local networks (LAN) cooperate with them. Within a few years, the basic restrictions: administrative (control of the number of computers sold), financial (drop of prices of personal computers), and technical (development of communication network) disappeared. Computers became commonly used tools in offices, companies, R&D institutions, universities, schools and even private homes, which still at the eighties seemed to be utopia. This apparently optimistic trend has some negative aspects though.

The fast development of knowledge and fascination with computers and possibilities they create, especially among the youth, is not accompanied by the awareness that computer technology requires not only professional but also moral qualifications from the users. With the rapid development of hardware and software market illegal software trade appeared. To certain extent it was due to the lack of the appropriate regulations in Polish law, which could have restricted this phenomenon. Only in February 1994, Polish Parliament proclaimed the act, mainly based on the EU legislation, regulating intellectual property protection, including computer software. It enables counteracting against illegal software and databases trade by administrative legal means. It cannot however stop copying both databases and software for private, non-commercial use.

So far Poland has been the country with a small number of typical computer offenses like breaking into classified databases or their destroying for criminal reasons. It is more common that computer viruses are being implemented through the infected media; still the scale of this phenomenon should not worry. Open access to computer systems due to their connection with MAN or WAN networks creates the possibility for growth of the number of such undesirable cases. It is necessary to fight these phenomena with both technical and legal means. It also seems crucial to create and promote the model user of computer systems: honest, responsible and professional. So far the users have been trained in technical skills, and moral and legal issues have hardly been mentioned. Considering the spontaneous growth of interest in computer technology among both young and middle-aged generations, the idea of honest use of computers will meet general approval.

The easy access to computer networks and information services creates problems which can hardly be expressed in moral categories regarding human behaviour. Commonly accessible regional, countrywide or global computer network is a universal means which enables individuals, professional groups, institutions etc. realization of the particular, predetermined by them, goals. These goals are sometimes secret, and if not contradictory, usually they are at least not quite common. The institution presenting itself through Internet WWW pages usually tries to create a positive image, neglecting its weak points.

The user looking for prospective trade partners would like to have information about their weak points. The computer network operator who invested certain financial means would like to achieve the highest possible profitability, paying no attention to the quality of information sent through the network. For the users of databases placed in the network the easy access is as important as the fact they are credible and updated. The authors of information included in databases would like the users not to violate the copyright while using the database. Computer technology, as any other technology, is in a way morally neutral. It is human behaviour, supported by technology, that can be evaluated from the moral point of view. It could be assumed that all subjects involved in the process of creating, storing, processing, sending, rendering, or using information through computer network realize their own goals, and the problem lies only in easy, common access to the network and its efficiency.

The advocates of such liberal attitude should be reminded that not all the partners playing "common access to information" game, have the same chance to win, and thus the play is not fair. Usually the user is the weaker partner and more often he becomes a looser. He must accept: financial terms of using the network and its resources, technical and formal constraints (e.g. restricted access to some databases), language barriers, etc. At the same time the users are usually not informed if the information provided is updated, complete, credible, precise, etc. They must take into account that the information could be irrelevant or exceeding their current needs.

On one hand, as the factor positively influencing global communication, the development of information services through computer networks is undoubtedly a positive phenomenon. On the other hand, it makes it possible to influence individuals or groups which are not always aware of it or willing to be influenced by others. The following list of morally doubtful or even illegal activities can be made:

a) imposing the unwanted information (advertising, propaganda, etc.) over the users;

b) spreading the false information (e.g. economic forecasts, address databases, wrong advisory services, etc.), which can cause losses;

c) providing low quality information which can substitute the competent one (e.g. encyclopedic entries, information on museum resources etc.);

d) spreading information violating personal interests of individuals, economic interests of companies, legally protected secret information, etc.;

e) spreading information violating moral or social order (promoting pornography, racism, offending religious or patriotic feelings, etc.).

Only in the last two cases the interests of the users as well as the other people whom the information concerns are protected by law. The first three cases can undergo moral evaluation but they are not regulated by legal acts. The question arises how to restrict the scope of these undesirable activities effectively.

Theoretically speaking, it is possible to fight the above mentioned undesirable phenomena using one of the following means:

i. technical,

ii. financial and organizational,

iii. legal and administrative,

iv. educational and social.

They will be explained successively.

i. The range of technical solutions is quite limited.

Computers do not understand the information they process, and research over semantic analysis of texts and images are still in the initial stage. That is why the computers cannot evaluate the merits and select the information. Technical means can only: assure (though not in 100%) the confidentiality of the information chosen and restrict the access to the network nodes, databases, etc. to the particular groups of users, select information according to easily recognizable formal or, to certain extent, topical criteria. Thus technical solutions can only support the other ones. The development of international standards, especially those concerning the protection of confidential information sent and stored in databases, as well as securing databases from illegal access, can play a significant role in the field of technical solutions.

ii. Organizational solutions are based on different access levels to the resources and to the services of the networks granted to various categories of users divided according to their rights. A similar, selecting role can be played by financial solutions, e.g. properly calculated scale of charges for services rendered by computer networks. Price reductions can help to stop the development of software black market. In fact these are preventive activities, contrary to the idea of common access to information. Introducing such solutions causes many problems: to make them effective they must be connected with technical solutions, they cannot be contradictory to law, e.g. to constitutional civil rights. Restrictions in access to resources and services of the computer network bring another problem: who should grant or refuse the rights, supervise if they are obeyed, judge the possible litigations, etc. Experience of Central and East European countries, including Poland, where the state claimed such powers, has been negative. What is more, it proved that the more restrictions in access to information or means of its spreading introduced, the stronger the trend to avoid or break them is. Breaking the rules becomes an entertainment, a challenge, a revenge for restrictions imposed, the matter of specifically understood honour of the user.

iii. On the contrary to organizational solutions, which are aimed against certain categories of potential users, the legal and administrative solutions concern particular individuals or organizations, who violated legal acts and thus have to bear responsibility through administrative or judicial procedure. These are proper and obvious solutions in democratic countries, where the law is based on the balanced interests of individuals and society. The problem appears, though, because civil (especially copyright) and criminal law in many countries is not precise yet in the cases concerning new phenomena which occur in connection with development of global means of communication and spreading information. For example, in Poland legal regulations exist forbidding to spread pornography, but no regulations state clearly what pornography is. Global range of computer networks makes it desirable to unify the law on criminal exploitation of computer networks in as many countries as possible. International organizations could play an important role here, popularizing the best legal solutions. It should be mentioned, though, that law does not regulate certain activities which can be called a "gray zone" of the undesired phenomena.

iv. Educational and social solutions are mainly preventive. They inform about inappropriateness or social harmfulness of some ways of using computer networks, even if they are not strictly forbidden by law. A positive role could be played by internationally proclaimed and approved Chart of Ethical Use of Common Information Exchange Means. The Chart should be widely promoted, and included in teaching programmes of secondary schools and universities if they are only anyhow connected with computer sciences. The atmosphere of acceptance for the Chart rules should be created among computer specialists and users, and, at the same time, of disapproval for individuals, institutions and companies which break those rules. Scientific, social and professional organizations could create a system of competitions and awards for those users and operators of computer networks who distinguish themselves with ethics, high quality of the information services offered, etc. In catalogues of network resources the databases characterized by the high quality level of the merits could be specially marked. In other words, the metainformation could be included in the resources of the network, which would enable the user to find the proper quality information at first. Constant observance of such procedures will gradually restrict the influence of worthless or harmful information.

3

Free Software

Digital information technology contributes to the world by making it easier to copy and modify information. Computers promise to make this easier for all of us.

Not everyone wants it to be easier. The system of copyright gives software programs "owners", most of whom aim to withhold software's potential benefit from the rest of the public. They would like to be the only ones who can copy and modify the software that we use.

The copyright system grew up with printing---a technology for mass production copying. Copyright fit in well with this technology because it restricted only the mass producers of copies.

It did not take freedom away from readers of books. An ordinary reader, who did not own a printing press, could copy books only with pen and ink, and few readers were sued for that.

Digital technology is more flexible than the printing press: when information has digital form, you can easily copy it to share it with others. This very flexibility makes a bad fit with a system like copyright. That's the reason for the increasingly nasty and draconian measures now used to enforce software copyright. Consider these four practices of the Software Publishers Association (SPA):

- Massive propaganda saying it is wrong to disobey the owners to help your friend.
- Solicitation for stool pigeons to inform on their coworkers and colleagues.
- Raids (with police help) on offices and schools, in which people are told they must prove they are innocent of illegal copying.
- Prosecution (by the US government, at the SPA's request) of people such as MIT's David LaMacchia, not for copying software (he is not accused of copying any), but merely for leaving copying facilities unguarded and failing to censor their use.

All four practices resemble those used in the former Soviet Union, where every copying machine had a guard to prevent forbidden copying, and where individuals had to copy information secretly and pass it from hand to hand as "samizdat". There is of course a difference: the motive for information control in the Soviet Union was political; in the US the motive is profit. But it is the actions that affect us, not the motive. Any attempt to block the sharing of information, no matter why, leads to the same methods and the same harshness.

Owners make several kinds of arguments for giving them the power to control how we use information:

Name calling

Owners use smear words such as "piracy" and "theft", as

well as expert terminology such as "intellectual property" and "damage", to suggest a certain line of thinking to the public---a simplistic analogy between programs and physical objects.

Our ideas and intuitions about property for material objects are about whether it is right to take an object away from someone else. They don't directly apply to making a copy of something. But the owners ask us to apply them anyway.

Exaggeration

Owners say that they suffer "harm" or "economic loss" when users copy programs themselves. But the copying has no direct effect on the owner, and it harms no one. The owner can lose only if the person who made the copy would otherwise have paid for one from the owner.

A little thought shows that most such people would not have bought copies. Yet the owners compute their "losses" as if each and every one would have bought a copy. That is exaggeration---to put it kindly.

The law

Owners often describe the current state of the law, and the harsh penalties they can threaten us with. Implicit in this approach is the su ggestion that today's law reflects an unquestionable view of morality---yet at the same time, we are urged to regard these penalties as facts of nature that can't be blamed on anyone. This line of persuasion isn't designed to stand up to critical thinking; it's intended to reinforce a habitual mental pathway.

It's elementary that laws don't decide right and wrong. Every American should know that, forty years ago, it was against the law in many states for a black person to sit in the front of a bus; but only racists would say sitting there was wrong.

Natural rights.

Authors often claim a special connection with programs they have written, and go on to assert that, as a result, their desires and interests concerning the program simply outweigh those of anyone else---or even those of the whole rest of the world. (Typically companies, not authors, hold the copyrights on software, but we are expected to ignore this discrepancy.)

As a matter of history, the idea of natural rights of authors was proposed and decisively rejected when the US Constitution was drawn up. That's why the Constitution only permits a system of copyright and does not require one; that's why it says that copyright must be temporary. It also states that the purpose of copyright is to promote progress---not to reward authors. Copyright does reward authors somewhat, and publishers more, but that is intended as a means of modifying their behavior.

The real established tradition of our society is that copyright cuts into the natural rights of the public---and that this can only be justified for the public's sake.

Economics

The final argument made for having owners of software is that this leads to production of more software.

Unlike the others, this argument at least takes a legitimate approach to the subject. It is based on a valid goal---satisfying the users of software. And it is empirically clear that people will produce more of something if they are well paid for doing so.

But the economic argument has a flaw: it is based on the assumption that the difference is only a matter of how much money we have to pay. It assumes that "production of software" is what we want, whether the software has owners or not.

People readily accept this assumption because it accords with our experiences with material objects. Consider a sandwich, for instance. You might well be able to get an equivalent sandwich either free or for a price. If so, the amount you pay is the only difference. Whether or not you have to buy it, the sandwich has the same taste, the same nutritional value, and in either case you can only eat it once. Whether you get the sandwich from an owner or not cannot directly affect anything but the amount of money you have afterwards.

This is true for any kind of material object---whether or not it has an owner does not directly affect what it is, or what you can do with it if you acquire it.

But if a program has an owner, this very much affects what it is, and what you can do with a copy if you buy one. The difference is not just a matter of money. The system of owners of software encourages software owners to produce something---but not what society really needs. And it causes intangible ethical pollution that affects us all. What does society need? It needs information that is truly available to its citizens---for example, programs that people can read, fix, adapt, and improve, not just operate. But what software owners typically deliver is a black box that we can't study or change.

Society also needs freedom. When a program has an owner, the users lose freedom to control part of their own lives.

And above all society needs to encourage the spirit of voluntary cooperation in its citizens. When software owners tell us that helping our neighbors in a natural way is "piracy", they pollute our society's civic spirit.

This is why we say that free software is a matter of freedom, not price.

The economic argument for owners is erroneous, but the economic issue is real. Some people write useful software for the pleasure of writing it or for admiration and love; but if we want more software than those people write, we need to raise funds.

For ten years now, free software developers have tried various methods of finding funds, with some success. There's no need to make anyone rich; the median US family income, around $35k, proves to be enough incentive for many jobs that are less satisfying than programming.

The Free Software Foundation (FSF), a tax-exempt charity for free software development, raises funds by selling GNU CD-ROMs, T-shirts, manuals, and deluxe distributions, (all of which users are free to copy and change), as well as from donations. It now has a staff of five programmers, plus three employees who handle mail orders.

Some free software developers make money by selling support services. Cygnus Support, with around 50 employees [when this article was written], estimates that about 15 per cent of its staff activity is free software development---a respectable percentage for a software company.

Companies including Intel, Motorola, Texas Instruments and Analog Devices have combined to fund the continued development of the free GNU compiler for the language C. Meanwhile, the GNU compiler for the Ada language is being funded by the US Air Force, which believes this is the most cost-effective way to get a high quality compiler. [Air Force funding ended some time ago; the GNU Ada Compiler is now in service, and its maintenance is funded commercially.]

All these examples are small; the free software movement is still small, and still young. But the example of listener-supported radio in this country [the US] shows it's possible to support a large activity without forcing each user to pay.

As a computer user today, you may find yourself using a proprietary (18k characters) program. If your friend asks to make a copy, it would be wrong to refuse. Cooperation is more important than copyright. But underground, closet cooperation does not make for a good society. A person should aspire to live an upright life openly with pride, and this means saying "No" to proprietary software.

4

Participation in the Global Information Society

Regardless of a nation's level of economic development; political, economic and social structure; and language and culture they are all seeking to develop and improve the quality of life of their citizens. At present, the industrialized countries have an overwhelming lead in development over most developing nations. However, modern information and communication technologies offer a significant window of opportunity for developing countries to accelerate their development in all spheres of economic and social activity and to narrow the gap between countries.

The world stands today on the threshold of a Global Information Society. This position has been arrived at through the truly remarkable advances that have been made in recent years in the development of ICT as well as the construction and development of national and global information infrastructure. Through these developments it is now both technically and economically feasible to bring modern information and communications technologies to any part of the entire world. Equally as important, people around the world, including those in developing countries, are increasingly demanding access to the emerging global information network. Hence, communities in Mexico, for example, have installed personal computers and built microwave towers to communicate with the rest of the world, allowing school children to interact with other students all over the world and keeping farmers apprised of both local and world crop prices. Also, India launched a programme to link its biggest cities with a nationwide network that will facilitate the dissemination of government information and provide an infrastructure for commercial applications.

The present Global Information Infrastructure (GII) has evolved from a research and development programme in networking that was initiated and funded by United States government in the 1960s. This programme, which sought to establish a decentralized telecommunications system in which an assortment of variously located computers could communicate with each other even when one or more parts of the system had been seriously damaged, was primarily designed to satisfy the military requirements of the United States. From these origins, the Internet has since developed into a global network of computer networks with many different types of users.

Realizing the full potential of the Global Information Infrastructure (GII)

As described by the Vice President of the United States of America at the first World Telecommunication

Development Conference held in Buenos Aries, Argentina in 1994, a major goal of the Global Information Society is to:

> ....build a global community in which the people of neighboring countries view each other not as potential enemies, but as potential partners, as members of the same family in the vast, increasingly interconnected human family.

The Internet today is a fast-growing, global network that enables people from all over the world to provide and access a variety of content, communicate with one another, purchase goods and services, and even co-ordinate complex, far flung worldwide activities at relatively low cost. The Net is estimated to be growing at a rate of 10-15% per month, with numbers rising from about 56 million Internet users worldwide in 1995 to about 200 million people in 1999. Also, its American origin notwithstanding, more than 50 per cent of current Net users at present are outside the United States and that percentage is rising; by 2000, less than 20 per cent of all Internet users are projected to be in the US.

At present, citizens and residents of industrialized countries enjoy good access to the Internet. For example, Finland and Iceland - first and second among countries with the most Internet hosts per capita - had 62 and 42 Internet hosts per 1,000 population, respectively, in 1997. At the other end of the scale, the information revolution has hardly arrived in Africa - the world's least developed region - where fewer than 15 countries had full Internet access in 1996. As a result of this situation, most developing countries have yet to assume a serious role in discussions on setting goals and standards for the GII. This should not deter them from seeking ways to ensure that their concerns and interests are included in the design, delivery, regulation and content of the world's information expansion. Clearly, a partnership between rich and poor countries is necessary in such an endeavour.

The potential benefits of the Internet for developing countries are well-known: namely that it presents exciting new opportunities to reinvigorate and accelerate the rate of economic and social development. However, the changes engendered by the Internet have been generally to the exclusion of the very poor people in developing countries that the Internet can particularly benefit. At present, the proliferation of the technology is restricted by the lack of appropriate infrastructure and the expense of computing technology. Hence, the dilemma for the average farmer in a developing country, say, would be to choose between spending about $3000 on the technology and approximately $20 - 50 per month on subscription fees or investing that money on farming tools, fertilizers or irrigation systems to produce a good harvest and an adequate income. Unfortunately, in nearly all cases in most developing countries, the question simply does not arise because the farmer lacks the necessary financial resources or access to them to enable him (or her) to use the Internet. Under these conditions, the race to effectively deploy the technology to increase productivity and promote social change and development may be over before it starts.

While it cannot be denied that top-level decision makers in some developing countries are not always convinced that investing in ICT should be accorded topmost priority, there is now at least a political will in many developing countries to support and encourage these processes. Much of this new spirit has been encouraged by industrialized donor countries and organisations such as the United States, Denmark, UNDP and the World Bank which have provided much financial and technical support to developing countries to strengthen and develop their national information infrastructure technologies. As a result, new legal frameworks and standards are being set up to promote the development and interconnection of national information infrastructures. In Ghana, for example, the basic policy instruments to encourage private investment and entrepreneurial activities to expand and enhance information technology has been put in place and the country has three licensed Internet Service Providers as well as five network services that provide mainly e-mail services.

Major challenges that confront developing countries in embracing modern ICT include the formulation and implementation of effective and practical strategies to enhance the capabilities of their populations to make the best possible use of information technology. Obviously, any country that wants to take full advantage of the opportunities provided by ICT will have to prepare its population to use the technology effectively. An obvious strategy to achieve this objective is to establish computer literacy courses. This may not be sufficient, however. Consequently, it will be necessary to ensure that these courses are complemented by teaching people - from primary school pupils, secondary school and university students as well as adult learners - skills to find information, critically evaluate it and also how to use it creatively to solve their problems.

A related objective is to ensure the effective application of information technologies to reduce, rather than widen and deepen social inequities or worsen inequality across the technological divide. Mechanisms to achieve this objective include, for example, public telecentres that have been promoted by the ITU as well as information service centres which are promoted by a coalition of private and public sector interests in the United States. These centres provide people with access to development-oriented applications and content as well as ICT-based facilities with associated training. Further, these centres can serve as the community libraries of the future and major instruments to achieve the goal of wide public access to the Internet.

Regardless of the sophistication of the technology or services being offered, a simple strategy to achieve these objectives could include the provision of assurances to potential users that they can allow the GII entry into their homes, workplaces and lives to access and share information safely and without forfeiting any of their rights. Governments, businesses and public-interest groups working together on information policy and content issues, must address these concerns. Equally as important, governments and the private sector must continuously seek to demonstrate in imaginative and practical ways the potential benefits of the GII to citizens, especially the more disadvantaged in society, for example, through tele-medicine or access to information on market prices for their crops. After all, it is only when people are exposed to, and see, tangible results of applications that they can begin to appreciate how the ICT can be used to improve their lives. This appreciation is the key to stimulating demand for the services and content of the GII, which in turn will provide the impetus to remove institutional and regulatory barriers to its full utilisation.

It should be noted that most young people, regardless of whether they live in rich or poor countries, will feel strongly motivated to learn and use ICT, from portable phones to the Internet. As a consequence all governments should place emphasis on educational programmes as a lever to increase the competence of the population at large.

Ethics and the development of the GIS

Decentralisation is an important characteristic of the Internet's culture and technology. Another important feature is that many Internet users view themselves as part of an "Internet community" that has its own culture, ethics and rules. We are all aware of "netiquette" as well as the existence of Internet jargon that has been developed by Internet users. As this community grows, many challenges concerning access and use as well as issues such as regulation, ethics and content on the Internet will confront policy makers.

There is a general consensus around the world that development of the GII and realisation of the goals of a Global Information Society will require concerted action and co-operation to develop a global information policy framework that will ensure, among other things, that:

1) the privacy of individuals and organisations using the GII is protected;
2) the security and reliability of the networks the information passes over are preserved;
3) the intellectual property rights of those who create the information, education, and entertainment content are protected;
4) that the content of information (particularly that of an intolerant, racist or pornographic nature)

circulating on the Internet and access to it, especially by children, is regulated.

Deliberations and action on all these issues must involve all countries represented by their governments, private sectors, labour, academia and the general public. Wide consultation involving all the major stakeholders should foster the formulation of a constructive regulatory framework that will be attractive to all and safeguard the interests of individual countries or groups of countries.

In these deliberations, the stakeholders must seek to avoid or iron out potential discrepancies. For example, an impending EU law that aims to safeguard the privacy rights of European citizens by setting common rules for the export and use of many kinds of personal data has an unintended consequence: a chance of trade conflict with the US. More generally, if exercised, the data protection directive could play havoc with global trade flows by cutting off companies' international communications networks.

Another concern involves the potential of ICT to have a negative effect on the social behaviour of users. For example, the range of services that can be accessed on the Internet is so comprehensive that it can, as stated by UNESCO, "unduly privilege the 'man-machine' relationship" to the detriment, on the one hand, of social intercourse and, on the other, the development of self-reliance.

At present, however, many of the risks associated with some of these phenomena are poorly understood and more detailed study and research is needed to enable policy-makers adequately consider the necessary actions, if any, that will be required to address the problems.

There is also considerable concern in many quarters about the maintenance of linguistic and cultural diversity. Given its origins in the United States as well as the dominance of the English language as a medium of international communication, 90% of the databases on the Internet at present are in English. Consequently, non-English speakers do not have effective access to the content available on the Internet.

However, there are few technical constraints on the development of databases in other languages that can serve the interests of a variety of local communities. Nonetheless, technology-induced globalisation is seen by many as a threat to local customs, values and beliefs. This is therefore an area in which further research.

Promotion of the growth and development of the Global Information Infrastructure and its use presents several challenges to all countries, perhaps most especially for developing countries.

Developing countries will, in particular, have to develop cheap, simple and robust technologies for coping with increasing numbers of users and traffic. In pursuit of this objective, research and development is required on the development of means for promoting equal access to cyberspace.

In addition, and as part of the overall strategy to achieve this objective, research will have to be conducted to identify and develop innovations to promote the use of ICT by different population sub-groups as well as to study its effects on society and development. An important topic that must also be researched is how ethical principles related to globalisation can be implemented.

5

Universal Access to Information Resources

Main Challenges to Universal Internet Access

Today, if we examine the apex of human development, we can bear witness to the birth of new 'tribes'. For the first time, skills, wealth and culture are forming the basis of preferences rather than the age - old kinship of blood ties and physical location.

We are indeed facing massive conflicts between blood ties and knowledge ties, where the new structures of knowing are far outpacing the ability of traditional governments, institutions and all kinds of other entities to process and respond to information.

Geographical boundaries are fast becoming barriers of no consequence. This is bringing about mass dislocation in governmental institutions around the world.

The transformation in the structure of global communications systems has redefined the basis of participation in development and modernity by creating new levels of entry into the global economy. Today, participation in the information economy has become the revised standard and fundamental precondition for economic development. The growth of the information sector in lesser industrialized countries is now the latest barrier in access to capital and development resources.

At the same time, universal Internet access holds great promise for:

- Significantly increasing the speed of achieving universal based on the achievement of universal access to Information, Communication Technologies (ICTS) and appropriate content and applications
- Decreasing poverty around the world - through the linkage of access to ICTs.
- Opening up global markets through Internet commerce to any individual or entity that can gain access to the Internet and to online communications tools.
- In the opening up and enabling of transparency in governance.
- Increasing the spread of democratization through increasing civic discourse and citizen involvement in government.

The Internet, unlike other media, represents a new collective mental space. It is critical to ensure that all societies gain the opportunity to merge their existing worlds into, and become a part of an expanded world - that includes the new virtual world. Leaving the creation of this newly expanded world of ours to technocrats, engineers and the sway of multi-nationals is a recipe for a world that we would not want to bequeath to future generations.

With the advent of the Internet, nations, regions, cities, villages, and individuals are able to work and to come together within global, networked communities based on shared interests at a speed and inclusiveness never before possible.

UNESCO can play a vital communications role in helping to educate and galvanize governments and the public at large to understand how fundamentally important it is to put into place a free public communications framework. One that is non discriminatory to all voices, commercial and non-commercial; and that ensures that adequate space on the network, regardless of technology, is reserved for undistorted - substantive forms of information, dialogue and debate. Universal access to the Internet will then be able to happen and to flourish through one critical mediating institution: namely, the institutional infrastructure of public space.

Universal Access cannot materialize as a reality unless and until specific key challenges are fully addressed:

The Right to Access Information

It is important to understand that lowering the barriers to Internet access is helpful to everyone in the context of gaining easier access to information. An argument can be made that every individual should have the right to access information - regardless of disability, economic situation, or geographic location. Without this realization there will be no consistent progress in the effort to provide global access. Global access itself is not enough. Cost of access has to come down to where not just the elite in emerging nations can afford to get on the Internet. The issues of inaccessible design should be addressed. Once the access is available then the content should be usable by all. Access to the Internet without the ability to use the content is a hollow shell. Access to the Internet without the ability to use the features or participate in e-commerce is nothing more than lip service to the idea of universal access.

The benefits of addressing the problems of inaccessible design extend to include all people, including the community of people with disabilities. (About 10% of the world's population is disabled, with a disproportionate amount falling into the poor population in emerging economies). It is imperative that there be some way to insure that people with disabilities in the developing world are not separated from everyone else. There must not be even more of a Digital Divide opened between people with disabilities and the efforts to provide Internet access to all in emerging economies. Once it is understood that accessible design is always in synch with low technology solutions, then big steps can be made to help everyone gain access to the information society.

Enforcing Accessible Design Solutions

Universal Design simply stated means that as many people as possible can use whatever process, object, or electronic or information technology that is being made available. By definition this includes low band width areas or the principles of Universal Design are not being adhered to.

This is the goal, not just for people with disabilities but for people everywhere. Below are some interesting examples:

Examples of Accessibility being Compatible with Low Bandwidth.

Users want to access any information they choose to look at as fast and with as little deductive effort as possible. One of the basic underpinnings of easily accessible web pages is good page and site design. This involves such things as, clear navigation schemes consistent placement of items on a page, and not using "leading edge" technology just for the sake of using it. Nowhere on sites that recommend good design, or anywhere on the W3C site (http://www.w3c.org) can one find recommendations that in and of themselves require high bandwidth to implement. In fact on the http://www.useit.com it clearly states that a web designer has from 10 to 30 seconds to grab and hold the attention of the visitor. Sites that do not load quickly as is suggested clearly do not fit into this category.

One of the easiest things that can be done to make a site accessible is the use of ALT (alternative text) attributes on image tags - When these attribute tags describe an image or tell its function, they can also provide information about the destination of a link. This effort requires no extra bandwidth and in fact in areas where bandwidth is low, the use of ALT attributes on image tags, allows a user who has turned off the images in their browser, or is using at text browser such as Lynx, to know what the image is, or what it does as well as the destination of a linked image.

To be accessible in a low bandwidth area, a site that offers a download of video of a speech should also offer a text alternative to the speech such as a transcript for example. In a low bandwidth area, this would be the media of choice.

The fact is that many people who attend tutorials on accessibility do so in part or in whole because they wish to use accessibility techniques to increase the usability of their sites in low bandwidth areas. According to Accessibility experts, in 99% of all cases, implementing accessibility techniques do not require adding substantial bandwidth to the needs of a web site - on the contrary, application of the kinds of accessibility techniques alluded to here, result in the reduction of bandwidth necessary to load web pages. People with slow modems and low bandwidth can access the electronic content of the Web even if they do not have the state of the art computer equipment. Likewise, people with personal digital assistants and cell phones can access the content of web sites incorporating accessible web design features.

Inaccessible design of information technology is a serious issue when it means that people cannot access many content sites on the Internet. It also means that people are encountering substantial software incompatibility with adaptive devices and other means used to gain access to the Internet. Today, there are now standards that should be enacted so as to ensure maximum Internet access for everyone.

Awareness of issues and solutions is critical to providing access to the Internet for people. A critical component of raising this awareness is a central entity (which could so well be UNESCO) that can provide outreach, education, standards support and a central repository for resources and solutions to access problems for those who need such information. This resource could also serve as a repository for global legal and policy briefs that can serve as models for laws and policies in all regions of the world where they are needed.

Issues

The main challenges related to extending universal access to information resources at a reasonable price are:

- General affordable worldwide Access
- Accessible Hardware and Software
- Accessible Web and Internet Features
- Availability of Accessible Internet Access devices
- Availability of Accessible Web Sites
- Accessibility of multiple languages
- Poor program design of software for users

Currently none of these items exist in enough quantity to provide the needed level of access. This access should be provided for all and the solutions specific to people with disabilities need to fit within the larger solution. Solving these issues is actually critical to providing global affordable access.

One little addressed fact is the level of computer literacy needed for performance of even common rudimentary tasks in day to day living. Users should not (as Alan Cooper states in his seminal work, "The Inmates are Running the Asylum" have to acquire computer literacy to use computers for common rudimentary tasks in every day life.

Solutions

The solutions listed below cannot be separated out from the overall solutions proposed for achieving Universal Access.

- Improve Infrastructure on a global basis using an affordable, maintainable structure
- Explore building accessible electronic and information technology features for services offered by Internet Service Providers
- Recognition of the right to access information regardless of disability, economic situation or geographic location.
- Raise Awareness of Accessibility Issues throughout the world with outreach and education.
- Encourage organizations working for the validation, management, and distribution of speech, text, and terminology resources and tools, and to promote their use within the global telematics RTD (research and technological development) community.

Today, there are areas that show some hope, for example, the European Union has accepted Web Accessibility Initiative (WAI) standards. The US on both a Federal and Local level is accepting standards to improve web and electronic and information technology accessibility for people with disabilities. Australia and the United Kingdom are instituting web accessibility regulations and Portugal has done so as well. Singapore has made huge efforts to include Internet access to all of its citizens, including those that are disabled.

These areas are models for the rest of the world. UNESCO could look to support these efforts and collect and disseminate the solutions as well as contributing to the solutions by outreach, and raising awareness of the accessibility situation. Having coherent "Best Practices" for this area that can be used by everyone. Further encouraging all players in the Internet arena to produce accessible solutions, be they makers of access devices, software or assistive technology, should be a goal of UNESCO. There should also be a Center devoted to collecting and disseminating accessibility solutions.

To accomplish global access and access to all content, outreach and educational programs should be initiated and sustained to raise the awareness of accessibility issues. The efforts of organizations like the W3C and the Internet Society's Internet Societal Task Force Accessibility working group are to be encouraged in this regard.

What type of global backbone and access system can support anytime anywhere usage?

Whatever system is developed it should be standards based in so far as it should be easy to use and economically viable to access this system with low cost devices and devices that support Assistive Technology.

The system should be based on the principles of Universal Design since it must as much as possible be usable by everyone not just a privileged few. (It should be noted that the advent of web on wireless phones may actually help to push the kinds of important design principles being talked about here.)

Infrastructure

The first area that should be addressed is the

Infrastructure issue. This may take many forms, such as wireless as in Tonga, or fiber, or satellite, or some other as yet not developed architecture. Whatever form it takes, it should be usable by a large number of affordable and access devices and devices using assistive technology. Much of this technology is being developed now.

As it is developed in the areas with higher economic standards, those areas should be encouraged to use that technology to help develop infrastructure solutions that are economically feasible for other areas of the world. The pay back for this of course is long term. As those areas develop access to the Internet and it services they will become more economically viable markets.

This infrastructure is a pre-requisite for all other aspects of access to the Internet for anyone. A required feature of the infrastructure will be access by a variety of standard economically affordable devices. (An interesting example of such an economic device would be closed captioning of television programs making it possible to index recorded video by captioning so that everyone benefits from the ability to search the associated captions for words of interest and then be in a position to play the associated video.)

Access Devices

These devices should be designed using the principles of Universal Design. Access devices should be designed to operate in a variety of modes such as audio, or video. This will benefit all those who operate in an environment that requires one mode or another. Ideally these devices will be multi-modal. These devices should also be usable with various types of assistive technology. Lastly they must also be affordable. Access technology that cannot be used by most of the world because of cost, is not a feasible solution. Public access centers, where people can use public facilities to access the Internet and its features, is one important solution. Properly developed and distributed, multi modal access devices will allow areas, which are mostly permeated by low technology, to access the information, which is stored on a high technology Internet.

Development of Content Information Networks

The dominant content of information networks in emerging economies should be comprised of educational applications and public information applications, rather than commercial applications that stimulate ever - greater demand for environmentally unsustainable consumer products. Community access for public services in the areas of health education and government services by means of public access points in the information infrastructure will help a great deal in the distribution of access to priority content of this kind.

Presentation of Content

Using the principles of Universal design and standards such as those developed by the W3c Web Accessibility Initiative, will allow the largest number of people to successfully access content on the Web This will allow access to content from almost any location and with almost any device. This is particularly important not just without advanced infrastructure to support high speed access, but it is also critical to accessing information using alternate access devices such as cell phones and

PDA's (Personal Digital Assistants). In the United States this is becoming a preferred way to access information for large portions of the population. In many parts of the world it may well be that wireless technology will become the most economical way to access the web. In some cases it may be the only way to access the Internet.

This adherence to the principles of universal design will also have to include non-verbal ways to communicate information as well as ways to present information in languages other than English. This is vital to the idea that the Internet is for everyone. Methods to easily translate or present content in languages other than English should be developed. Translations that are verbal as well as written should be provided. In addition non-verbal methods of conveying information must also be developed for those who cannot read, or who have other learning problems.

For example weather reports can be vital information to farmers who may not necessarily be able to read. However they still have a right to access the information to receive information vital to their existence.

Ways need to be found to present this information in low bandwidth areas, places where access maybe via alternate devices, or to an audience that may not be able to read. These types of presentations are crucial to the successful implementation of an Internet that is accessible to all people.

Encouraging Placement of Content on the Internet in Native Languages - other than English.

Many governments are aware that the lack of content on the Internet in their native languages, is a serious impediment to Internet use in their countries. Even in the developed world, the preponderance of English on line poses a serious obstacle to universal access. For example the Government of Canada has pointed out as recently as 1999, that 31.2 % of Quebec Net surfers speak only French, and that this is an obstacle to use of the Internet.

Governments should be encouraged to work on an integrated strategy with regard to the presence and quality of their native language/s content and services on the Internet. The European Union's MLIS (Multilingual Information Society Program) offers interesting insight into European efforts to promote linguistic diversity and stimulate the provision of multilingual services etc.

The question of placement of a critical mass of content in languages other than English is a fundamental issue to address whenever the issue of universal Internet access is in question.

The Storage of Content

The ideal way to store content is as a separate entity and then tailor the presentation to the audience. This could be translation to another language, graphical or verbal presentation for those who cannot read, or must have an audio presentation of the content, or almost any other presentation imaginable. This of course is an expensive way to store and present content and will not be economically feasible to most people who wish to present information on the Internet.

The next best thing and far more practical is to examine ways of building this capability into the devices that access the Internet. While this does place the burden of providing this capability on the producer of the device, it also spreads the cost out over a much larger area. It also allows the user some flexibility in choosing the type of device that best suits their particular situation.

If content is produced in a way that adheres to such standards as are being developed by the W3C Web Accessibility Initiative, then there will be a much better chance that it will be usable by a large and diverse audience regardless of disability.

The use of these standards needs to be encouraged. As a first step, UNESCO could put together a review series online of "Best Practices" and keep it updated. This could be based on current work being done and on the current standards. Just as This would be similar to what Bangladesh has shown with their micro-credit and village cell phones, - both of these efforts show imaginative approaches, which can easily bring the poor into the e-commerce Internet loop.

As a second step UNESCO could sponsor an international center to gather public domain solutions to various accessibility problems involving Electronic and Information Technology. Just as the European Union recently accepted the Web Accessibility Initiative (WAI) for web pages, the UNESCO Accessibility Center could serve as a global central clearinghouse to help promote and disseminate accessible electronic technology of all kinds. This center could also run outreach programs teaching accessibility techniques and workshops on legal and policy issues dealing with accessibility.

Creation of Repositories of Basic Information

UNESCO should seek to create repositories of basic information that can help improve and assist nations in their development. This information should be stored and presented in ways that are usable by all people including those who cannot read.

A good start would be for the UNESCO to also encourage the United Nations to make sure they also set an outstanding example.

UNESCO could design these repositories so they are usable in low bandwidth areas as well. From the point of view of language in general, it will be important over time for UNESCO to put into place on its own web sites, access to text to speech converters capable of working in multiple languages.

They could contract with a non-profit organization to build and maintain these repositories or they could build them themselves. Private industry, governments, and foundations interested in improving access to information on a global basis could jointly fund these repositories.

The Internet Society and other non-profit organizations could manage and co-ordinate these efforts on a worldwide basis. Among other efforts would be a translation effort to disseminate knowledge from one language base to another.

It is not reasonable to assume that everyone will speak the same language and the only way to improve two way communications is to be able to translate information on both and auditory and text basis.

Development of the above type of technology is already in its infancy. With the advent of worldwide access to computers it should be encouraged. To a limited degree this can be accomplished today through the use of database and XML technologies. These efforts could be encouraged and enhanced for this type of project.

With server based repositories set up to serve many different areas in many different ways no one area will be left out, no one person will be left out as long as they have some type of Internet Access. These repositories should be designed for access by any type of device in any type situation. They should follow Universal Design Principles mentioned earlier in this chapter. This will insure that whatever technical situation the user who wishes to access the information finds themselves in, they will be able to use the repositories. (By implication information needs to be stored in many different forms to accommodate variations in access speeds and costs, for example.)

In many rural situations access to basic information such as weather and other time critical information, and to local and national government information, can make a huge difference. This type of repository can hold information to help improve the technical base in many areas, not just in computers, manufacturing, agriculture, and other basic areas where the sharing of information can lead to economic improvement.

Since it is not realistic to expect great improvements in Infrastructure on a global basis in a short time frame, it is more likely that server based repositories can be designed to serve these areas with the infrastructure that exists. To be available as the access situation is improving as well. This is a solution that can adjust to any situation in which the user may find themselves. This will basically allow low technology to access high technology and will grow with the improvement of Internet access in regions around the world.

The Importance of Supporting Audio Communications

Bringing out the Importance of Audio Communications illustrates the importance of bringing focus to bear on audio communications via the Net, to start with: audio "dumb terminals" (the telephone, radio) are more or less universally available. It is also becoming apparent that many advanced methods of accessing the net will use audio and other modes of access. These methods can be used to improve the techniques of access on a global basis in environments where what is considered traditional access may not be feasible. At the same time, it is critical to not only find a way for all people access such Net content, but also to be able to produce content for placing on the 'Net themselves. The Net cannot be a one way communications device, and all who access the net should be able to share their ideas in one way or another.

To insure this there needs to be simple clear mandates for accessibility regarding all public information put out by Governments for the information of their Citizens. The same information should be contained in important Guidelines to all other Internet users to bear in mind as they construct web sites and databases for online access by fellow Internauts.

The Impact of Open Source Software (OSS) in Emerging Economies

The impact of open source software in less developed countries can result in:

- Easy access to software products. Open source software can be easily available for individuals and companies in less developed countries.

- Cost-effective transfer of software technology. Developed countries can make cost-effective contributions to less emerging economies by helping them to adopt free software technologies. Since there is no royalty or per-copy fees, the cost of this transfer is really low for the contributor country. Contributions can be focused in training, localization and contextualization with a great multiplier factor.
- Direct access to software technology. Emerging economies can be granted access to leading edge software technologies without having to pay expensive royalties.

Issues of Accessibility and Bandwidth in the Context of Socio-Political Evolution.

Evolving political and structural institutions typically produce deregulated markets in many emerging economies. However, incumbent network providers (telephony or otherwise) either retain large power (cases like Telmex in Mexico, Telgua/Guatel in Guatemala), or are acquired by much stronger international companies (witness C&W in Panama). Therefore, governments have to apply efforts in order to promote competition with a goal toward equity for the benefit of the general population.

Bandwidth does not arrive on its own. The market for bandwidth provides a profitable business to Incumbent Local Exchange Carriers (ILECs) and again governments have to press for its provision in open markets.

In countries where favorable forms of deregulation are incipient, it is recommended that governments make every effort to develop more access to health, education and government services by means of public access points in the information infrastructure at low or no cost, with clearly defined rules.

The rapid rise and evolving compatibility of cellular and other mobile communications gives governments and companies extraordinary opportunity to encourage the development of wireless devices with full Internet access in order to provide immediate enhanced access to the Net for mobile users. Tenders and auctions for promoting wireless devices should be considered urgent. So should be the development of content designed for access through these devices and oriented to education and training or their support and continuation in the workplace.

Accessibility rises only in the context of a political and cultural evolution, which promotes respect among people, enlightens and sensitizes people to the critical problems of others and creates new job opportunities for the emerging new economies.

Telecommunications Deployment

More than a century after the emergence of telecommunications, developing countries still do not share in the benefits of a universally distributed basic telecom service. Extension of existing and new telecom networks to rural and lesser economic zones will be the necessary condition of any participation the Information Society.

The new information technologies are cheap and becoming cheaper - but not without cost. Communication networks are cost effective when being implemented for large populations; the primary challenge is the initial infrastructure investment. Countries with low or low-density populations cannot afford the initial costs associated with advanced communication infrastructures. Hence they require partnerships with the private sector as well as other investment. It is however often the case that the most modern telecom equipment is often cheaper today than the older equipment; so it may well be the right decision to acquire and put into place new telecom equipment.

Regulatory Frameworks and Information Infrastructure

The regulatory framework in developed countries enforces protection of investment, intellectual property and individual privacy in the information market. The legal framework addresses private sector involvement, skilled human resources, standards and implementation. In most emerging economies regulatory frameworks concerning information do not exist.

Although the rapid growth in information technology is changing methods of doing business at home, at work and in organisations in both developed and emerging economies, regulatory frameworks have had very little effect on emerging economies.

While information technology, including telecommunications, has penetrated every market in the developed world, emerging economies still view information technology as a means to support management information systems, finance and accounting facilities, and data processing. Computer penetration per capita in both China and India in the area of small office/home office (SOHO) is still not significant in relation to population numbers.

Telecommunications still remain a major issue in almost all emerging economies. In the context of countries like China and India, if information infrastructure were to cover the widespread Chinese and Indian populations and technology were to be made available to access global information through the

Internet, then the economic scene would be revitalised. Awareness of the Internet and its importance for policy makers exists only at the executive level, but unfortunately, not at the political level. This needs to be addressed urgently in such populous countries .

The Current "Digital divide": Implications of Restrictive Telecommunications Regulations.

A growing difference in the levels of market liberalization in the supply of Internet access service is leading to one form of "digital divide" on the global scale.

Many countries have introduced or are introducing telecommunications regulations that discourage the development of Internet access service through competition.

Granting monopoly in Internet access service to a national incumbent operator or charging high license fees for the Internet access service are examples to barriers of market entry. Most of such regulations are found amongst emerging economies.

At the same time, many some emerging economies have introduced incentives to encourage the use of the Internet. For example, some countries in Latin America provide incentives to reduce a retail price of PSTN for the access to the Internet. The supply of Internet access service is free from a regulatory burden in the majority of developed countries.

It has become evident that the IT-use in economic activities, especially the use of the Internet for a variety of economic transactions, such as electronic commerce, has stimulated positive impact on the national economy. This has been demonstrated by the recent economic growth in the US.

As Internet use in business activities substantially contributes to economic growth in general, the gap in economic development will widen between those countries where end users enjoy the benefits of the Internet, without financial or any other obstacles, and those where they do not. This difference largely coincides with different national telecommunications regulatory regimes, i.e. those countries that are open to competition and others that are not, as the regulations create costs to Internet users and service providers. Thus, telecommunications regulations create a "digital divide" in economic development on a global scale.

Telecommunications Deployment

To address the question of telecommunications deployment, it is useful to consider a closely related question: what makes the Internet different from other telecommunication services, such as those which run over the public switched telephone network (PSTN), There are arguably a number of differences.

Although there is a similarity in the underlying technology of the Internet and telecommunications services; (both the Internet and the voice telephone network run over the essentially the same wires) but the equipment attached to those wires, and the use made of them is different.

On the Internet messages are broken down into digital "packets" of data which means that the wires can be used much more efficiently, to carry a much higher volume of information, at a lower cost. The dilemma occurs over pricing.

Pricing

The public switched telephone network has traditionally been priced on the basis of usage. By contrast, the dominant pricing principle that has evolved for the Internet is flat rate pricing. The model for wholesale pricing differs too.

A service provider terminating a particular telephone call receives a fee for doing so. By contrast, on the Internet, there is almost no flow of cash on an end-to-end basis. On the telephone network, emerging economies are net recipients of financial flows, but on the Internet they make net out payments for carriage of their traffic.

Traffic flows and value flows

In most telephone calls, the traffic flow is approximately even between the caller and the called party. But with web browsing, the traffic flow is highly asymmetric with the main flow being towards the party, which originated the call, who also gains most value from the call.

Advent of Internet Telephony

Another area of serious concern in the context of telecommunications services and the deployment of those same services over the Internet, is the advent of Internet Telephony. This presents the biggest dilemma for PTOs. On the one hand, it promises to reduce the price of international telephone calls for the citizens of the country. But on the other hand, Internet Telephony could be viewed as a threat to the pricing structure of the incumbent PTO and undercut its profitable business in originating and terminating international calls. The bottom line is that protectionism is not what works, so it is actually important that PTO's look at the advent of Internet Telephony as a global opportunity rather than as a local threat.

Emerging economies are trapped between the need to attract private capital (general international capital) to upgrade and expand their telecommunications network, on the one hand, and development goals on the other. The case of India is perfect for illustrating how this trap can derail the most powerful of developing country economies. Unless development goals in information infrastructure are recognized as legitimate and necessary at the international level (such as the World Trade Organization, (WTO), with risk guarantees provided by global institutions such as the World Bank, few nations will escape this trap.

International investors will continue to boycott telecom markets where development goals are imposed on operators and providers. Such goals could be universal access, education, health, etc. The reality is that trade law which governs the telecom services market often does not explicitly make concessions to development goals. Thus governments must undertake at their own initiative the construction of a nationwide network of public access points both for telecommunications and the Internet. Most simply cannot afford the cost. As countries realize that technological and communications advances constitute the driving force for social and economic betterment, the lack of telecommunications infrastructures has major implications for global competitiveness and economic sustainability in a networked world.

Common Misunderstandings about the Nature of Internet Service

In the area of Internet services, many believe (mistakenly) that :

1. Since there is the over- concentration of Internet backbone business in the USA, with no requirement for the operators there to share costs of leased circuits, that this means that ISPs in other countries must in most cases pay the entire costs of two way links.
2. This situation is further aggravated by the high costs of leased lines from the countries concerned.
3. The end result is that Internet providers and users in the United States gain free Internet access to rest of the world at the expense of other countries, including the poorest of them.

This line of reasoning reflects several misunderstandings about the nature of Internet service. To begin with, there is an increasing amount of local or regional "hubbing" that reduces the need to obtain pairwise international connection to US backbones. Moreover, an increasing amount of content is being found locally and is of high value, especially when it is in the local language. More important, however, is understanding what Internet service is and in particular, the difference between private or public peering and the offer of transit service on the Internet.

Peering is not Free

Every ISP must assure that any packets sent by customers will be delivered to the destination any where on the Internet. There are two ways to achieve this goal:

By buying international transit service from a third party and reselling it or by arranging for a sufficient number of local and international connections to achieve global connectivity by means of pairwise exchange of traffic between the customers of the pair of "peering" ISPs. Peering is not free. It costs money to create the necessary connectivity. Indeed, it may well cost much more to achieve connectivity by means of peering than by purchasing transit services. The transit service must deliver received traffic to any internet connection in the world. While the purchaser of this service need only deliver traffic to customers of the purchaser's network. The burden of cost lies with the transit Internet service provider.

It is primarily for this reason that international transit services providers position their service offerings to recover the cost of international access circuits. It is also important to keep in mind again that "peering" is not free. There are significant costs associated with achieving sufficient connectivity to allow global service on the basis of pairwise peering. International Internet service providers must recover those costs to sustain their business.

As the economics of Internet service provision continue to change with time - as costs come down and as connectivity increases, it will be useful to revisit cost recovery mechanisms for all ISPs to determine whether changes in traditional compensation are appropriate.

The Need for Next Generation Internet

With regard to the next generation Internet, including mobile Internet, the need for vastly increased Internet IP address space has made the transition to Internet Protocol version 6 (IPv6), (which provides far more addresses than current version 4,) a matter of urgency.

The European Commission intends to take several steps to facilitate, where appropriate, the timely transition of the information economy to the IP addressing system. This will include the timely introduction of next generation Internet addressing (IPv6).

ISOC's support for IPv6, is not inconsistent with its support of universal access for all - in terms of what it is actually going to cost to governments and private enterprise, to push for this next generation Internet protocol, and to ask that products be shipped IPv6 ready. Having researched this matter with IPv6 experts, the Internet Society is very aware that the transition from IPv4 to IPv6 will be a significant challenge and that it will take some years to fully implement. The vendors of router equipment and of computer operating systems into which IPv6 capability should be placed have not felt strongly motivated by their customers to move more rapidly on implementation of IPv6. It has become apparent, most especially at the recent INET2000 in Yokohama, that mobile Internet access may prove to be the primary driver of need for the larger address space inherent in IPv6. It is anticipated by the mobile telephone vendors that on the order of 1.5 billion Internet-enabled mobile telephones will be in the market by 2004. Adding to that the continuing growth of personal digital assistants, laptops, desktops and various world-wide web and e-commerce servers, and one has a recipe for running out of IPv4 address space in a few years.

The use of Network Address: Translation devices has been shown to be flawed by the Internet Architecture Board because it interferes with important end to end functions including encryption and digital signatures that are critical to successful e-commerce development. Consequently, the Internet Society and its technical branches are strong proponents of movement in the industry towards the newer IPv6 protocols.

The Importance of E-Commerce to Emerging Economies.

The Internet can level the competitive playing field by allowing small companies to extend their geographical reach and secure new customers in ways formerly restricted to much larger firms.

At the same time, however, there are significant barriers to the participation of SMEs, (Small and Medium-sized Enterprises) in the global electronic marketplace:

- Lack of awareness of electronic commerce
- Lack of suitable products and integrated systems
- Lack of a sound legal basis, combined with the newness and continued evolution of the market Complexity and cost of electronic commerce, and uncertainty about its benefits and security, are perceived as significant barriers and obstacles to the use of electronic commerce by SMEs.

The growth of electronic commerce should have great significance for emerging economies, allowing them to participate more actively in the global economy. Indeed, some believe that information and communications technologies can serve as mechanisms enabling emerging economies to "leapfrog" stages of development.

A recent study found many areas in which Internet could strengthen economic policy programs: economic research and analysis, public transparency and advocacy, professional networking, institutional networking, distance technical assistance, distance education, regional approaches and business-oriented Internet programs.

Payment Standards for e-Commerce.

There are currently no payment standards for e-commerce. There is a global trend towards increasing usage of credit and debit cards as payment tools for goods and services sold on the Internet. Electronic cash has failed to find a standard and is out of use everywhere. Smart cards have not yet reached the necessary critical mass. Electronic order of physical goods to be paid on delivery is popular for internal trading in some countries.

As a result, countries without a well-developed and pervasive system of plastic money cannot benefit easily from electronic commerce.

Tax Jurisdiction Issues

The key problems of how to tax Internet transactions arise from three areas:

- Existing taxation collection mechanisms do not work for electronic transactions -- evidence gathering is almost impossible.
- The lack of global agreement on what taxation to impose on Internet transactions and how to collect such tax payments. Already, Internet tax havens are springing up worldwide.
- Existing definitions of commercial transactions often do not apply to electronic transactions, rendering taxation authorities totally hamstrung.

Perhaps the single biggest problem is the issue of determining in which tax jurisdiction a particular transaction takes place. Most taxation authorities rely, by and large, on the physical evidence of a transaction to determine which taxation authority has jurisdiction over the transaction in question. However, with Internet commerce, the buyer, the seller, the point of transaction, and the actual provider or fulfiller of goods or services can be in different countries. Because there is no physical evidence, it is difficult to make a tax ruling.

The Economics of Internet Connectivity

In the beginning, all aspects of cost for the Internet were

borne by the US Defense Advanced Research Projects Agency. When the NSFNET (National Science Foundation Network) was created, the US National Science Foundation bore the cost of operating the NSFNET backbone network. Universities and research institutions bore the cost of networking their respective campuses/buildings and NSF subsidized the founding and operation of the intermediate level networks (such as NYSERNET, SURANET, MIDNET, BARRNET and so on). NSF also sponsored the interconnection of non-US research networks to the NSFNET backbone through an International Connections program operated for NSF by Sprint.

Similar kinds of government sponsorship are to be found around the world, augmented with a variety of non-profit cost-sharing arrangements, such as those leading to the formation of EBONE and NORDUNET, for example.

Each ISP would exchange routing information with the other connected ISPs and this information would serve to pass traffic between the commercial customers of each of the ISPs by way of the paths connecting each participating ISP with the CIX(Commercial Internet Exchange). The exchange of such routing information was called "peering" because each of the ISPs effectively acted as equals or as "peers". No charges were made between the peering ISPs on the basis that each ISP received equal value from the exchange of traffic with its peering partner.

Commercial Peering

The US Government endorsed the practice of commercial

peering when the NSFNET backbone was retired in 1995. (Note that the ARPANET backbone had long since been retired in 1990). The formal establishment of Network Access Points (NAPs) by the National Science Foundation formed the basis for a competitive collection of Internet backbones to interconnect and exchange traffic - assuring full Internet connectivity in the US that had formerly been assured through interconnection with the NSFNET backbone.

Observers often misunderstand that peering is somehow cost free. Nothing could be more untrue. To understand this, it is vital to appreciate that "Internet service" means that a packet sent by a customer can be delivered to literally any possible destination on the Internet. (To achieve this connectivity, an ISP either has to arrange to be connected to a sufficiently large number of NAPs (or peering points or Internet exchanges) and/or engage in sufficient direct (peer-to-peer) network interconnections to assure full connectivity. Or the ISP must purchase what is called "transit" service from another ISP that IS fully able to route traffic to any destination in the Internet.)

A new ISP often starts out by purchasing transit service from another ISP (e.g. a backbone service provider) and re-selling this service to its customers. As the ISP grows, it may negotiate peering arrangements with other ISPs either at NAPs or by direct (or "private") peering in addition to purchasing transit service to reach those destinations not reachable through the peering interconnections. It is important to note that whether the interconnection between ISPs is accomplished by peering or by purchase of transit service there is cost to the ISPs either for the cost of connecting to a NAP, establishing a private peering connection or purchasing transit service.

The Economics of Establishing Peering Relationships.

Generally speaking, ISPs agree to peer if they conclude that it is more cost effective to pay the cost of access to a common NAP and then to exchange traffic between their customers than it is to achieve this same goal by purchase of transit service. The cost of transit is reduced because some of the traffic is now diverted to the peering streams, but there IS a cost for the peering, namely the cost of access to one or more exchange points. Typically, peers interconnect at multiple NAPs or with multiple private interconnections to assure reliable operation. The balance between the cost of transit and the cost of peering is one element of the economics of Internet service.

Full Internet connectivity is established by any particular ISP through direct connection to customers, through peering relationships and through the purchase of transit service. A large ISP might achieve full connectivity through a combination of peering and direct customer interconnection without the need for purchasing transit. Because peering has costs, it is usually the case that only an ISP with a sufficiently large revenue base can afford to utilize peering and customer interconnection as the exclusive means of achieving full Internet connectivity.

Economics and Internationalism

As telecommunication prices for leased circuits drop, domestically and internationally, more options are opening up for ISP interconnection. In recent months, nearly two -thirds of traffic originating or terminating in

Europe is kept in Europe while two years ago, two-thirds of the traffic originating or terminating in Europe went to the United States. This is also indicative of the grown of web-based services in Europe - providing more local sources of information than ever before.

Historically, international Internet transit services have been purchased by ISPs outside the US by connecting international leased lines to US Internet Service Providers. The factors leading to this architecture are changing.

As international service prices drop, more regional interconnections can be expected, reducing costs for servicing out-of-region traffic (more will stay in-region, less has to go outside the region). Regional networks are already emerging in Asia, Latin America and will eventually emerge in Africa as well. Moreover, global Internet Service Providers will be able to offer transit services on domestic links, reducing the costs to resellers considerably.

A Note on Monopolies

For many years, telecommunications services were the province of monopolies chartered in each country. To achieve international telephone and communication services, one simply had to agree to interconnect the monopoly telephone services of each country on a bilateral basis (setting aside cases where one country relays traffic to a third party). There was no choice in the matter. If country A wanted to be able to exchange traffic with country B, there was no question about having to interconnect the unique monopoly networks of country A and country B. Each monopoly would have paid its costs for the half circuit connecting them and then negotiated a so-called settlement rate that each monopoly would charge the other for termination of traffic. In many countries, high settlement rates have meant that the telecommunications companies were bringing into the country substantial revenues.

Furthermore, if international communication services are in the purview of a single monopoly provider, competing ISPs within a country, to the extent they must rely on international connections to achieve full Internet connectivity (e.g. through purchase of transit services on international links), are potentially at risk.

The monopoly service provider can charge whatever it wants for international circuits linking to transit service providers. The situation is exacerbated when the same monopoly provider also competes for business from end-users.

This scenario only underscores the potential value of domestic competition to drive down costs, including costs for international service.

In the presence of competition between carriers in country B, it is no longer a foregone conclusion that any particular network in country A must connect to all of or even more than one of the networks serving customers in country B.

The settlement system is giving way to pairwise business negotiations between telecommunication service providers who have a choice of interconnection partners.

Competition in the domestic and international telecommunications markets has had a powerful effect on the costs of operations both for Internet services and more generally for telecommunications services.

The Economics of Emerging Economies

The term "emerging economies" brings along with it many connotations. Consider a new ISP just starting out in country Z. The ISP will need to rely on local telecommunications facilities provided by local telecom providers or it will have to put into place its own facilities to reach its customers. To achieve full Internet connectivity, it will need to connect to at least one and possibly more than one ISP capable of delivering transit service to the rest of the Internet.

Historically, customers for international transit service typically pay the full cost of the circuit linking them to an international transit ISP. While past history has favored US-based ISPs for this service, thanks to the relatively low costs for international services in the US, the rapidly evolving infrastructure in other regions of the world are permitting new ISPs to connect to transit services on a less-costly regional or even domestic basis.

Equally important is the expansion of global Internet backbone services on a highly competitive basis. The global backbone providers have points of presence in many countries and regions and the cost of the international circuits are subsumed within the cost of operating the global backbone.

Consequently, there is sharing of these costs among customers and the prices are subject to vigorous global competition.

Furthermore, unless local rules prohibit sharing of circuits, consortia of ISPs could share the cost of a regional or international transit service circuit. Or a single ISP could purchase the transit service and resell it to downstream ISPs, reducing the average cost per ISP.

The formation of local peering points (packet exchanges) can potentially reduce costs by allowing new ISPs to exchange traffic among their respective customers for the cost of access to appropriate peering points, reducing the absolute capacity needed for international transit service. All of these scenarios suggest that the historical model of pairwise interconnection of monopoly carriers is giving way to a richer mesh of interconnections among competing service providers in local, regional and global settings. These trends should lead to reduced costs for Internet services everywhere, including the emerging economies.

Where telecommunications infrastructure is lacking, there are several paths to bridging the so-called Digital Divide. One is to make deliberate government investments in infrastructure (e.g. through loans from the World Bank, through the UN Development Program). Another is to establish a business climate in which foreign and domestic capital is available and competition is encouraged so that substantial resources are brought to bear on the problem of developing infrastructure.

Among the surprises in Internet economics is the observation that a country can take advantage of Internet for business purposes even when the Internet is not widely deployed in the country. For example, India has a modest but growing Internet infrastructure, but in cities such as Bangalore, there are many well-educated engineers who have strong Internet skills. These engineers use the Internet to export their designs or their outsourcing services to other countries where Internet is more widespread. In a sense, this is a bit like exporting talent without having talent leave the country. This can certainly help to reverse the brain drain. It is a portent of a globally competitive future.

Roles and Responsibilities of the Public Sector

While national information policy in emerging economies concentrates on trade, international relations, national security and technology, very little attention has been paid to accessing information electronically through the Internet and to deriving benefits.

Emerging economies, in order to achieve faster economic growth, should include in their official documents high-priority plans for implementing electronic information delivery systems. Policy statements should be integrated into national planning documents such as five-year plans and should be implemented on schedule. Sufficient funding should be allocated at the planning stage and should be made available quickly for implementation.

Emerging economies will need to pursue a balanced approach to the information sector, maintaining an emphasis on development goals even while remaining within the powerful constrictions of international trade law. According to a key Internet Society member expert in this area of research, Dr. Shalini Venturelli, it is vital that these economies evolve effective mechanisms to promote and enforce the public interest function of communications industries in serving education, social and cultural development, and public-opinion formation.

In the absence of such institutional and legal mechanisms, the information sector will tend to serve the high end user market, the advanced information service needs of multinational industries based in these countries, and the international content industry seeking expanded markets for their cultural and information products in categories such as film, television programs,

Internet Services, news, books, magazines, and data services, ultimately resulting in full-scale commercialization of conventional and digital networks. It will be difficult if not impossible to retrospectively impose public service, development-oriented obligations, once the emerging information sectors of developing nations have been thoroughly integrated into the structure of global commercial communications.

Innovative Uses of Hybrid Technologies to Build Telecommunications Infrastructures.

It is recommended that emerging economies, in particular, consider the use of hybrid technologies to achieve universal access; this is important when the costs and timeframe associated with building infrastructures are prohibitive. For example, low cost packet switch technologies can be implemented with a small scale radio transmitter, a cheap sound card and a Linux PC with radio modem software (a small, 9600 baud modem is implemented in software and is usable on very low cost personal computers).

With more economical resources available, low cost 80-to-110 kbps radio modems can be considered as technology options to more expensive infrastructures. With low speed access, server technologies can be used effectively. Content rewriting, online compression, active caches can all be used to increase the perceived transmission rate. Very low bit rate audio and video can also be effectively used in this context.

Broadband is more difficult, but it should be considered that even in industrialized countries high-speed interconnections are not always feasible at low cost. Lower cost hybrid technology options emerging in the marketplace include utilizing satellite technologies, television signals, and the Internet to produce innovative, lower cost options to providing greater access at lower costs.

Although lower cost at the component level, the costs associated with developing innovative hybrid technologies lie in the requirement for skilled systems integration technologists to design, implement and maintain these infrastructures. The key to successful implementation is investing in sound design and planning.

All efforts to improve access to the Internet infrastructure such as wireless or other access should include the requirement that devices using this type of access should be usable with standard types of assistive technology, or include these technologies in the devices themselves. Ways to encourage this type access should be found and incentives to providers should be supplied to keep the cost within reason.

UNESCO's Potential Role in Identifying & Showcasing Best Practices UNESCO could put together a review series online of "Best Practices" and keep it updated. (For example, Bangladesh has shown important successes with their microcredit and village cell phones - both of these efforts show imaginative approaches which can easily bring the poor into the ecommerce Internet loop.)

Access to knowledge is fundamental: basic principles are based on easing all the three points mentioned above (access, use, and creation of knowledge). There should be equal access to technology for creating communication links. If possible, interconnections through research networks should be eased in terms of economical access, interconnection equipment, skills needed to create the connection and routing.

Access to open source software and knowledge should be organized and, if possible, localized. More co-operation should be sought out by the many projects actually running: UNESCO, EU, etc. with duplicate and competing efforts. UNESCO could contribute to the solution significantly by assisting in the development of a repository for all Internet "Best Practices" worldwide.

Promoting the Concept of Libraries as Centers for Global Information Access.

A corollary is that UNESCO can obtain large effects for its efforts if it promotes an accelerated education for librarians in matters of information and communications technologies, (known as ICTs).

They can be effective change agents, as has already been shown in countries like the US and France, but in the developing world they are in a situation of lack of resources, low self-esteem, and very poor technical knowledge. Establishing the concept of libraries as centers for access to information and, not only book repositories, will undoubtedly have a large result in a relatively short term.

The Importance of Telecenter Initiatives

The Internet Society thinks that promoting telecenters in emerging economies around the world, is an important step in helping to achieve significant steps forward in making access to Internet and Internet services more general, especially in rural areas.

As a result, it is specifically working on implementing self-sustaining Internet training centers in regions around the world. This will eventually allow the population in these countries to keep pace with developed countries, as it will give them access to technological and academic information as well as Internet training at a variety of levels.

The benefits they gain will affect every aspect of personal and professional life and enhance efficiency in administrative, educational, cultural and economical levels.

The Self Sustaining Internet Training Centers, (SITC) project, initiated by the Internet Society, is based on a close partnership and cooperation between local authorities, members of local Internet Society chapters and other relevant organizations involved in the development of the country or area in which the centers are set up.

The Internet Society will be asking for all community efforts such as mobile or static SITCs, should include some standard assistive technology as part of their access efforts. Examples would be voice input, screen readers for the blind and those who cannot read, and technology to help people with mobility impairments to access Internet features, especially the Web and email.

Examples of Areas Notable for Telecenter Activity

A major effort in Telecenter activity can be seen in

Tunisia. Since October of 1998 the Tunisian Government has been putting into place tens of "Publi-centers. The key purpose of this effort has been to make access to Internet and Internet services general throughout Tunisia, especially in rural areas and to create jobs for young university graduates.

The Tunisian Government's overall approach to information technologies aims at giving the largest possible number of people access to modern means of telecommunication.

This has been achieved through reductions in phone and Internet access rates in combination with promotion of the use of Internet among families, the opening of public Internet access centers and concentration on placing more and more Tunisian content and Tunisian ecommerce web sites online.

In Latin America, a number of Telecenter initiatives have flourished and a few of them, notably one in Peru, are already providing extraordinary services. It still is true that the collaboration of academic institutions, particularly universities, is vital for projects in emerging economies.

As an example, some of the most effective Telecenter initiatives in Mexico are undertaken by UAM (Metropolitan University, Mexico City) with a small number of public libraries, and in a joint project among UNAM (National University of Mexico), Universidad Tecnologica de Tecamachalco and ISOC Mexico for rural/ small-town conditions. The main focus of these kinds of efforts are to:

- Promote regional or language-based multinational efforts to establish online offerings of minimal, common-denominator curricula.

- Promote online offerings of technology training for the general public.
- The availability of live online tutors, at least interacting through email, could be very useful.
- Scouting the best offerings available from universities, schools and similar institutions for training on and through technologies
- Conducting workshops to establish and diffuse cutting-edge concepts in lifelong learning the shifting landscape of professional and technical study and the models for open and distance learning.
- Promoting sustainable, self-financing endeavors of schools and universities in continuing education and extension, through an exchange of "Best Practices".

Consortia for the exploitation of excellence centers have proven to be a good way to use the locally available resources (for example, a local link or university). Examples of these research networks include the European Center for Excellence and the various exploitation and exchange centers. Community facilities can be employed if they are significantly low cost. In this sense, portals and information centers are better than large-scale infrastructures. Of great importance is the lifting of legal impediments and allocation of resources in a quick and low cost way (for example radio spectrum allocation).

One should look at existing research and advanced training facilities already available in emerging economies and enhance them through easier and less bureaucratic access to funding for equipment, academic exchange travel. And Diaspora populations, whose interaction with the receiving institution are enhanced by distance-education media and procedures, as well as scholarships and fellowships for students. If implemented successfully, this strategy can result in the creation and development of important links between universities, think tanks and the private sector.

Research networks in emerging economies can achieve much and should be aided to defeat significant obstacles.

It is recommended that countries with weak legal frameworks cooperate to define international standards. These policies include allowances for cryptography and legal acknowledgment of digital signatures to protect consumer and privacy rights.

Legal Barriers

1. In May 1998, the UNCTAD secretariat issued a study entitled "Electronic commerce: Legal considerations" which reviewed many of the legal issues raised by paper-based legal rules: the requirement for a "written document", "signature" or "original", the evidential value of electronic messages, the storage of electronic messages, documents of title and negotiability, allocation of liability, validity and formation of contracts and incorporation by reference.
2. Many of these issues had been raised in prior studies by the United Nations Economic Commission for Europe (ECE) and have been dealt with in proposed national and international instruments, the most significant of which is the "Model Law on Electronic Commerce".
3. In addition to the concern about paper-based requirements as a barrier to electronic commerce,

there is also concern that lack of harmonization in the rules generally applicable to electronic commerce would also result in effective barriers to trade. Areas that have been identified as involving legal issues relevant to electronic commerce include data protection, taxation, customs duties, security and authentication, intellectual property rights, liability of Internet service providers, illegal and harmful content, Internet governance (more specifically, domain names), electronic payments systems and consumer protection.

4. In the case of countries that lack appropriate infrastructures, the ability to prioritize international cooperation for the deployment of communication networks, promoting technology transfers and sharing communication resources satellites and others should be reinforced through strong policies and effective implementation actions

In conclusion, multiple solution sets are emerging for online access. Each case needs to be evaluated and customised to meet individual country needs. Priorities should be determined, depending on available resources. Indigenous resources should be harnessed and other resources tapped, including funding from international organisations and private enterprise.

The Internet itself needs to be used to mobilize support among specialized ministries, universities and industries to produce and manage information, and to emphasize institutional arrangements to influence policy makers and information purveyors to promote the Internet for the country's development. The question of access to the Internet for all people including those with disabilities are closely tied to all other issues involved with deploying a global and affordable Internet that is usable by all. These issues cannot be separated and the questions of accessibility and the solutions involved will improve access for all at the same time.

The benefits of addressing the problems of inaccessible design extend out to all areas of the world where lack of telecommunications infrastructure and bandwidth pose serious problems. Most importantly, the fact is that accessible web design enables low technology to access high technology, thereby contributing to a stable, sustainable electronic infrastructure. People with slow modems and low bandwidth can access the electronic content of the Web even if they do not have the state of the art computer equipment. Likewise, people with personal digital assistants and cell phones can access the content of web sites incorporating accessible web design features.

Unless basic laws concerning telecommunications enforce the making of Internet access as part of the basic services offered by governments and local governments to their citizens, other moves will be very difficult, and subject to ad hoc negotiations.

Given the pervasiveness of electronic information, access to ICTs is becoming a pre-requisite for people to enjoy many of the rights established in the Universal Declaration of Human Rights. As information is recognised to play a central and strategic role in everything we do, from politics to banking, from education to consumption, from the organisation of the state and the socio-legal system to organisation of culture and self-identity, it will become necessary to start debating a political settlement on the fundamental principles of information rights, just as debates to secure human rights and environmental security have gained some incremental ground in human awareness during this past century. This is indeed a future potential role for UNESCO to consider as it strives to find the best solutions to the problems of Universal Access at the dawn of the 21st Century.

6

Information Highways in Developing Countires

The Issue of Information Superhighway

The issue of information superhighway is currently mobilizing globalized attention. This attention is by no means solely confined to the Western developed countries; no less amount of concerns are identifiable in many of developing countries as well. Indeed it has become a world-scale topic.

Behind the evolving notion of information superhighway lies the sheer conviction that speedy adoption of digitalized information infrastructure and establishing a linkage with globalized information networks will provide a strategic imperative for promoting the nation's political democracy and socio-economic development. Developing countries are no exception to this globalized rush for the historical trend of "information revolution," allocating a large portion of financial resources to this end, regardless of their persistent lack of economic, industrial, financial and other social bases.

It is true, though, that the dream of developing countries to build up a modernized national information infrastructure as an essential technological basis for leap-frogging into affluent and democratic societies is sometimes confronted by skeptical questioning of its own validity in reality. Critical assessment of the informatization of developing countries displays in many instances not so much satisfactory consequences. The installation of advanced information infrastructure in the context of developing nations more often than not brings about not so much political and social benefits as system maladjustment. The socio-political potential of information technologies is least likely to be automatically realized in developing areas of the world.

If this is the case, what is called for is that a comprehensive and systematic evaluation of the conditions of applicability and possible consequences on the whole society must accompany the actual installation of advanced information facilities. Important is not the hasty involvement in the adoption of information technologies but systematic analysis of the conditions by which the potential benefit of informatization can be realized.

One of the most central issues related to the information superhighway project lies in the topic of the public's "universal access" to the information infrastructure. The issue of universal access and service centers around the policy concerns to extend the usage of information networks to the general public on a non-discriminatory and affordable basis. The idea contains the hope to ensure electronic democracy by enabling the public's equitable participation in the newly emerging information environment.

If we consider the agenda of universal access as a question of equitable participation of the general public in the nation's informatization infrastructures, the traditional notion of "universal access," originated from the experiences of Western societies, seems to contain some biases that are prone to restricting the scope of discussion about the informatization policies. More than anything else, the concept apparently carries the connotation of technological determinism in that top policy priority is placed on the provision of technological access. The concept of universal access carries an implicit theoretical assumption that the key to the successful realization of information society lies in the adequate provision for the widest public the "access" to information technologies.

The experiences of developing countries, however, teach us that the technological accessibility alone cannot easily open the way to the realization of a democratic and participatory society. In other words, the problem of information society does not solely exist in the matter of technological provision.

This chapter will suggest some lessons earned from the informatization processes of developing nations. It will focus on the question of how socio-political factors have caused major hindrance to the actualization of technological potential of advanced information infrastructures. More specifically, this chapter will propose a critical assessment of the informatization of Korean society, which has been deeply involved in diverse projects for introduction of advanced national information infrastructure since the inauguration of the Ministry of Telecommunication in 1994. By doing so, we hope this chapter can suggest some policy guidelines for many other developing countries eagerly pursuing the adoption of advanced information technologies. It is also hoped to propose a variety of practical and theoretical questions concerning the issue of digitalized information superhighway in the context of non-Western societies.

Disarticulation of Information Sectors

Amin (1982) and Evans (1979) mention that economic dependency causes the "disarticulation" of the periphery's structure of technology, social conditions, and the whole national economy. According to Amin (1982), the peripheral economy is, as a result of distortion, composed of sectors and economic entities that are not effectively integrated into an "autocentric" whole, but merely juxtaposed. Each sector of the national economy is to exist as an atom, independent of the others, preventing the economic activity of one branch from generating a "leading effect" on others. Disarticulation frequently takes the form of severe sectoral disparities, characterized by a fundamental absence of basic industries and a predominance of non-productive branches.

Serious disarticulation can be easily documented in the realm of national information infrastructure of developing nations. A certain sector of information infrastructure can be over-valued as compared with others, and the society can over-allocate resources to that sector at the expense of others, producing a structural gap within the development pattern of national information infrastructure. This is more or less a widespread problem confronted by many developing countries. Sussman reports that the actual employment of information technologies in developing countries is "geared mainly for prestige, with little regard given to long-term or social benefit."

This trend often leads to the disarticulation of information sectors such that, despite the overall underdevelopment of the sectors of information infrastructure having a greater public nature, developing nations are dedicated to installing the most advanced, expensive and computerized high technologies and international satellite link-ups, with the consequences of overdevelopment of elitist, advanced, and internationalized sectors as opposed to the retardation of less elitist, public, and grassroots sectors of information infrastructure.

In this regard, the Korean way of informatization also reveals a similar problem. As compared with the nation's deep and ardent commitment to the project of national information superhighway shown by the allocation of tremendous amount of financial resources to this end (Ministry of Telecommunication, Korea, 1996a), far less than a parallel amount of policy attention has been directed to more public sectors of the nation's information infrastructure. As an unavoidable consequence, even the metropolitan capital city Seoul has a very coarse public library system as compared with other capital cities.

This startling discrepancy between developmental levels of different information sectors gives rise to some important policy issues. Overemphasis placed on advanced and elitist information sectors at the expense of more basic, public and grassroots sectors can result in the reinforcement of existing gap between the information rich and the poor. Some critics may claim that greater policy emphasis should be laid on the construction of public libraries in order to provide the general public with more basic and essential information services, instead of allocating a vast amount of financial resources to the highly advanced and internationalized information superhighway project.

Similar patterns of disarticulation can be found in many other dimensions of the nation's overall information infrastructure. It is quite frequently happen in Korean society that a public organization's adoption of a digitalized information network tends to be utilized disproportionately more for bureaucratic and administrative purposes than for the its originally advocated public service functions. As an example of this kind of disarticulation, it is very common in Korea that newly introduced computers at public schools are exclusively monopolized by administrative staff members and not effectively utilized for the purpose of teaching.

The disarticulation of information sectors identifiable in the processes of informatization in developing societies proposes a variety of theoretical and practical questions. To begin with, disarticulation problem can lead us to question the validity of policy priority given to the advanced and digitalized information sector in the context of developing nations. It can be reminded that the substantial capital investment needed for the installation of sophisticated information networks requires the allocation of a large amount of financial resources for a developing nation, often resulting in the predicament of balance-of-payment shortage and augmenting foreign debt.

The second issue related to this disarticulation problem concerns about its effect of gap-widening between the information rich and the poor. The access to the advanced, computerized, and internationalized information networks are very likely to be limited to the information rich. And the pursuit of informatization of developing countries emphasizing the elitist information sector is also likely to result in the overequipment of most advanced and elitist technology at the sacrifice of more basic and public sectors of information infrastructure, thereby deepening the information gap.

Third, because digitalized information networks are ready to be incorporated into global information infrastructure such as Internet, the primary function they can serve is to work as the conduit for the unidirectional information dependence of developing nations on highly developed countries. This hypothesis can be easily confirmed by the tendency that, due to the underdevelopment of national information service systems, Internet users in a developing country are heading for international sources of information instead of national sources.

In sum, the problem of disarticulation raises the possibility that the top policy priority given to digitalized information superhighways by a developing country may not result in the fulfillment of the dream of socio-economic consequences in reality.

Networking from Above

The optimistic dream in regard to the coming age of informatization easily extends to the hope that digitalized information superhighway will provide a technological infrastructure for the promotion of participatory democracy. The hope usually stems from the expectation that advanced information technologies can make contribution to empowering of the grassroots sectors and serve as a backbone of democratic public sphere. According to this view, digitalized information technologies can help facilitate more informed and interactive public debates by enabling the mobilization of people's voices, especially those of the information poor. The era of information superhighway, this line of thinking envisages, will be characterized by more efficient public intervention in the political decision making processes.

However, the real world experiences make us very cautious about the suggestions raised by those who believe in this sort of technological determinism. One major hindrance to the full-scale realization of the technological potential for participatory democracy seems to lie in the traditional authoritarian political culture of Korean society. Critics like Yun argues that, contrary to the Western societies, technological introduction of on-line information networks alone cannot lead to the realization of participatory electronic democracy in Korean society where the long-standing authoritarian political tradition has suffocated the culture of free and open political discussions.

A close look at the actual ways in which Korean people use computerized networks frequently reveals the lack of the culture of rational public debate. People's actual pattern of telecommunication network usage is to a large extent limited to non-political and non-public purposes.

Discussion forums for public concerns are the spaces least likely to mobilize the public's participation. And even the communication taking place in them usually is not very likely to produce lively submission and exchange of opinions and ideas.

This might suggest that the public space generated by information networks are not so much successful in mobilizing people's public voices. The social culture of silence and underdevelopment of the cultural basis of rational debate seems to suppress the technological possibility of participatory democracy.

Another factor responsible for this general failure in the mobilization of the public's voice through digitalized information networks seems to be the government-initiated, centralized and authoritarian policy for informatization. The Korean way of informatization has been chiefly initiated and guided by the nation's central government. The nation's informatization process has been in a certain sense imposed on the civil society by the government, resulting in "networking from above".

The strategy of networking from above taken by Korean central government has made the national information infrastructure less responsive to the information need of civil society. Information networks in recent Korea tend to lack carefully designed services to encourage the citizen's suggestion of opinions about public matters. Public policy information serviced by public offices is also very limited in terms of both quantity and quality. Even the publicized information by a pubic office tend to be framed more for propaganda than for genuine information service for the public. Under these circumstances, it would be a rational choice made by the majority of network users to remain as passive consumers of entertainment than as active producers of political demands.

Communication Endogamy and Communication Closure

The original meaning of the term "communication" reminds us of the horizontal nature of human communication. The term, according to Cherry, originates from the Latin word "communico," meaning "to share." From this perspective, insofar as we are in a genuine mode of communication, we never simply send or receive messages, but always hold them in common. Communication by definition denotes inter-communication, a two-way process of interaction and mutual understanding.

This conception of communication also describes the principle of liberal democracy. The modern concept of democracy rose from the notion of open and free marketplace of ideas, within which a variety of opinions is publicly voiced and freely contended, finally culminating in the formation of the true and rational public will. The essence of modern democracy abides in the vitality of free and open discussion between contending views. The facilitation of free and full inter-communication between different social groups enables them to be transformed into the "democratically organized public".

Given that the original ideal of human communication lies in the horizontal exchange between multifarious and often competing social groups and meaning systems, genuine communication must occur across social boundaries and between multiple realities. This line of reasoning supports the idea that the sound basis of a society depends on the liveliness of "communication exogamy" as opposed to "communication endogamy." "Communication exogamy" refers to communication across particular social boundaries of any kind, while "communication endogamy" refers to communication within them. The former is typically two-way and transactional, while the other implies a one-way and oppositional.

When these two concepts are applied to Korean society, the predominance of communication endogamy over exogamy becomes obvious. Phenomenological examination of Korean society suggests the existence of a multitude of isolated and closed circuits of communication at every level of society. And each of these closed circuits being a communicatively self-sufficient and independent; not very effective social communication flows across these mutually isolated closed circuits. Endogamous communication seems to be the main rule.

The dominance of communication endogamy implies the functional breakdown of communication channels between social units. The possibility of open, free, and interactive flow of communication between autonomous social unites tends to be severely damaged. As a devastating consequence of the "communication closure" brought about by communication endogamy, a desirable social function of communication to unite and network the parts into a purposefully cooperative whole is to be severely undermined.

Communication endogamy, as a logical consequence, does seem to undermine the technological potential of digitalized information infrastructure in Korea. Under these circumstances, the introduction of modern computerized communication network services cannot effectively facilitate open flow of communication between diverse social sectors and governmental units, thereby inhibiting the possibility of mutual cooperation between them based on the exchange and sharing of information.

As an example, the pattern of computer network participation in Korea shows a contrasting discrepancy between the case of associations based on shared interest and that of forums designed for public discussions. Korean network users show only a lowest level of participation in the latter as opposed to their vitalized involvement in the former. In many cases, the linkages between autonomous computerized information networks display severe underdevelopment.

In this situation, the expected open and free flow of information between organizations and groups with the aid of computer networks tends to be cut off by their selfish sectionalism and other habitualized closure-oriented practices.

This tendency apparently suggests that the functions of modern computerized information superhighway are shaped and determined not solely by its inherent characteristics; but only in conjunction with the pre-existing structure of social communication. Thus, in order to achieve a full-scale actualization of information superhighway's technological potential, the general plan for national informatization should pay enough attention to non-technological factors at the same time.

Critical discussion about the consequences of Korean way of informatization suggest that the dream of information society cannot be realized by technological possibilities alone. Besides the technological side, the experiences recommend us to consider social, political, and other factors at the same time. The discussion gives us an obvious lesson that for the full-scale actualization of the technological potential imbedded in information highways, we should perhaps consider some socio-political factors more seriously. Frequently this non-technological factors are working as serious barriers hindering the free, open and multidirectional access to information in many developing nations.

Non-technological barriers can take a variety of forms within a society. For example, the information sectors of a country can reveal serious disarticulation with each other. In this case, the advanced information sector cannot be easily "networked" with more basic and public ones, thereby undermining the sound basis for the universal access to the information highways for information have-nots.

The connotation that information highways are not sufficient for the public unless supported and networked with "information local roads" or even "unpaved trails." In addition, special attention must be given to pre-existing social communication structure of a society. When communication endogamy prevails a society diverse social sectors, interests, voices, and visions cannot be properly networked and mediated. Political factors can add much variation to the shaping and usage of information superhighway.

The recognition of the central influence played by non-technological factors leads us to another lesson that the pursuit of informatization should be dynamically fused with a more general plan to reform undemocratic socio-political situation of a given society. The project of informatization should go hand in hand with a prospectus to reform a society's the overall authoritarian communication structure in order for the project of information superhighway to be more amenable to human needs and social necessities.

Finally, if we can agree that simple provision of technological accessibility to information superhighway cannot effectively ensure proper utilization. The issue of information superhighway poses the important question of how we can establish a ground for free, open, interactive and democratic networking of diverse social sectors.

7

Information Society in the 21st Century

Digital information and the proliferation of networks for its delivery are accelerating the emergence of the 'Information Society'. Its technical development and widespread use have, however, outpaced consideration for security, privacy, and the ethics of the production and dissemination of content. The prospects offered today by both the multimedia traffic and the millions of users accessing and transmitting digital information have also prompted the creation of large multinational conglomerates and agreements to exploit the resulting market potential. All of the above aspects need now to be addressed in order to make appropriate recommendations for their handling.

Historical background

Nature and its evolution mechanism is an analogue process based on complex multilevel interactive matrixes. The nearest natural event that resembles a digital evolutionary step are large scale environmental phenomenons or disasters. Man is part of the analogue evolution and is in itself an analogue machine, consequently "Scientific and Technological" developments for the greater part of human existence tended to be of the same nature. The advent of electricity changed that tendency in a drastic way and opened up new scientific horizons in a very short historical period of time.

Digital evolution

The first large scale use of digital technology was not for processing or computing needs but for communications purposes in the form of telephone exchanges, even if at the time in a mechanical form using relays as digital switches. Thermoionic valves in turn replaced the relays for the development of computing technology and the transistor replaced these as science progressed in its search for faster and smaller means to exploit the digital potential. Although faster and smaller it is still the technology in use today.

Digital revolution

The fact that we are now witnessing a digital revolution is not in doubt, what is more difficult to pinpoint is whether the emergence of a single event or digital technology has acted as the catalyst that triggered it. Five elements are considered to have contributed to this revolution :

- The conversion of the telephone exchanges to all digital technology and traffic with the conversion of speech to a digital (PCM) stream at the exchange input.

- Fibre optics
- Packet switched networks
- The advent of the personal computer
- Large low cost memories both semiconductor and magnetic

This digital revolution is causing the complete reassessment of the way the telecom industry and the information content industry see their future developing. That both now consider the world as their oyster is clear but while the former is very slowly beginning to think that perhaps " The digital Traffic " on their pipelines rather than "Time" is THE future business and not discriminated by content, the latter considers this revolution as a world gone mad and their current perception is that once they make available their copyrighted content on the networks it will be left to the mercy of the users and abusers with no control on the revenues or their copyrights. To complete this first phase of the digital revolution and usher in the information society era it is necessary for two things to happen, ONE is to replace the current phone sockets with a 2 Mbits digital interface box and TWO the price structure needs a drastic U turn. First it must in a short period of time be geared to the traffic on the pipeline in terms of digital quantity and not according to time elements related to distance and second it must be affordable to all. The cost of the information itself will be dictated by market forces as it has always done.

Freedom of information

An often quoted and equally often misquoted statement to mean many things and to suit specific occasions and arguments. Perhaps the most widely accepted version of "Freedom of Information" mean the freedom or the right of any individual, organization or institution to publish with a view to inform others any information they choose by any means they deem appropriate. The implied proviso is that they also assume the relative consequences of any such publication, like libel suits and even criminal prosecution.

Equally an even stronger belief bordering on a collective neurosis postulates that no government or other body, elected or not, must interfere with this "Freedom". The information industry at large has since it was recognized as such always strenuously defended this principle.

This digital information side of this industry is at present growing exponentially and the quantity and availability of digitized information is growing at the same rate, the financial interests and the lobbying power to ensure that this freedom is maintained keeps pace with the industry's growth.

Interference with the "Freedom of Information" principle means external and internal controls, legislation, selective exclusions and all of these applied within individual national boundaries to a dissemination media like digital information which has no geographical restrictions.

Socially unacceptable information will always be published and disseminated no matter what efforts are being made to prevent it and like any other unacceptable product the only way to eradicate it is for society to stop buying it and therefore cause the "manufacturers" to either go out of business or change the product line. Simple in theory; impossible in its expectation.

Privacy and confidentiality

Private information

Private information or information of a private nature as distinct and not to be confused with confidential information, copyrighted information and information security is more appropriately dealt in debates and congresses on human rights rather than information dissemination via communication networks as privacy is a right that every person is entitled to and nobody should take it upon itself to break such right. Unlike copyrights privacy has received little attention in debates within the context of networked information, even the more traditional channels of communications pay a limited lip service to this issue and then they touch only the periphery of it. Any debate on privacy must have as a central argument the case of what is considered as private information and irrespective as to whom it applies to whether the holder of such information has the right to divulge it for whatever purpose. Invoking the cry of freedom of information to private data should not be permissible in the information society. Once available on the networks as digital information any information can no longer be considered private and it becomes de facto either freely available or confidential and subject to the applicable security rules and legislations.

Confidential information

Confidential information is often confused with private information. This type of data is collected/required for specific purposes and needs for personal , social and business requirements. Medical, credit, financial records or any records which contains personal records on individuals are already covered by some form of data privacy legislation or other in most countries. It is curious to notice how on forms requiring confidential details the option box giving the right to reuse that data is invariably presented in very small print hidden at the bottom of the form. And that when it is present at all. Confidential business information however does not enjoy such protection and it is up to the company concerned to ensure its security of storage and access.

Security

Securing information content digital or otherwise is an old and widespread concern and its practice involves all three principal aspects of information, storage, access and the transmission media (Networks). The security aspect is dırectly related to the information content and the nature of the providers and their user population (ie military, corporate, commercial). Security is also an integral aspect when dealing with private and confidential information. There are also varying degrees of security ; within the context of public networks like Internet any information requiring a high level of security should not in principle be on the network at all.

However there are some information elements within the communication transactions that should not be readily obtained by third parties (ie passwords and financial codes), if the information itself need to encrypted that it begs the question of what it is doing on a public network in the first place, or the converse why is the network so insecure and accessible by unscrupulous anonymous individuals as to warrant such drastic and expensive measures to protect one's intellectual property. Perhaps a more lasting solution is to ensure that all network users are clearly and uniquely identified at all time and at every step of their activity on the network and the use of illegal or system commands are monitored and allowed only by authorized personnel. Any unauthorized use of certain commands should ring loud bells in some control rooms. If not done already. Excessive use or need for security limits the use and increases the cost of the system and consequently has repercussions on the revenues potential. In the almost 30 years that the professional online dissemination services have been in operation there has never been the need to protect the use of the system beyond an access password. Perhaps their modus operandi should be taken as a reference model for the Internet.

The Information Society

Ten years ago computerized information was still an arcane art limited to those in the computer and database production profession and to those users called then information retrieval specialists whose task was to search the computerized records for the data pertinent to their business activities. Information was still more of an art than a business. This is not to say that the existence of such computerized information technologies and search capabilities was unknown to the rest of the professional communities it was just that it did not yet touch them directly, it was still something that somebody else did.

The moment the personal computer began its inexorable conquest of every working desk is when " Information " reached society at large and can be said to have acquired an awareness of its own. Information awareness created the need to communicate it, to exchange it, information in fact developed an irresistible urge to travel the rapidly expanding digital highways. The personal computer became a repository of information and every PC user became a de facto information specialist, society now knows the consequential problems and benefits associated with storing retrieving and transmitting information .

Digital Information in the newly acquired societal awareness encompasses all aspect of daily life from speech to images and created a new term to define it " Multimedia ". The advent of the PC distorted the regular linear progression of the modus vivendi between science, information and society, there exist now a kind of symbiotic relation between the use that society at large makes of the technological development of computer science and information science. This new relationship appears to have speeded up the intellectual capacity in our everyday working life by increasing our ability to do more complex things in a shorter time and more efficiently.

The beneficiaries of the digital revolution

If this revolution was put on trial the defense would claim that everybody in the whole world is benefiting from it, while the prosecution would claim that in effect the defense is confusing between the part of society being exposed to it or having knowledge of its existence and the other part who actually benefits from it and that this division is applicable in varying proportion to all nations, developing and developed alike. The benefits of the digital revolution can additionally be classified as direct for those earning a living and making a profit from producing and delivering " Information " and indirect for those who, in a position to pay, use it in their daily professional and private lives. Then there is the rest of society who has a remote vision of this revolution in as much as it is limited to see only its results and its use in the availability of public information and some consumer products. There is no such thing as free digital information as there in no such thing as free communication, digital or otherwise. The most significant emerging parameter however is the spectacular growth in information traffic and the communications networks to carry it, this has lead to an equally spectacular growth on the part of communications carriers and owners of large " private " network of mergers, acquisitions and cooperative ventures to consolidate their relative positions in the global marketplace and to be thus better able to exploit the universally predicted Multimedia revolution.

In the same manner and for the same objectives the publishing industry and the online information services are slowly gravitating toward a small number of large conglomerates. The domination of the market place will then be monopolized by few and it is not difficult to predict that the divide between those who can afford to be in the information society and those who cannot will get wider and wider. Unless minority interests both in term of information content and social groups are openly debated, considered and protected. By suitable legislations if necessary.

Ethical considerations

In theory networked digital information knows no

borders or boundaries. It travels free and it is available to everybody . In practice it is more controllable than any other media. Nations can create filtered entry and exit points, monitor its traffic and identify content sources and so can the network providers, corporations and institutions. The fact that it has not been widely done so far does not mean it cannot be done, the tools are all there. When we talk about applying ethical considerations to digital information we imply control, of the content, its access and of its dissemination .

This in turn impacts directly on the freedom of information argument and who controls the application of ethical rules, will this monitoring be done nationally or internationally , by the application of legislation or through semivoluntary rules by the three principal groups in this game, the network controller, the information dissemination services and content providers any of whom can veto information content they consider unethical.

And who controls the controllers That some ethical rules on certain classification of digital information content should be considered and tabled as agenda items for debate is not in question, their eventual approval and application may prove however to be a veritable legal and social minefield.

The world of digital information is slowly spiraling toward large concentration of power bases. On the one side the network providers who are de facto monopolies whether privately or publicly owned and on the other side the services and content providers who through mergers and acquisitions are rapidly becoming sectorial monopolies in their own right. With this scenario in front of us the ethical legal and societal aspects of digital information are in danger of being sacrificed on the alter of commercial profits and the catch phrase" Responsibility to the shareholders ".

An equally important aspect is the loss of valuable information that is not considered profitable especially in the scientific technical and cultural areas. The flow of information in the emerging Information Society was seen as the foundation to create a more level social playing field. It is instead fast becoming a divisive and dividing factor widening the gap between those who can and those who cannot. This congress should address these issues as a mater of urgency so that the emerging information society as envisioned by the world leaders is not held to ransom by monopolies unethical information content and practices and afforded only by the few.

8

Searching on the Web

The web can be an incredible tool for professional development—for finding resources and information, latest practices, for participating in discussions with colleagues and independent experts, and for mentoring opportunities. But the rapid pace of change online makes the amount of available information quite bewildering. This chapter offers some suggestions for good research techniques, and for evaluating the credibility of the results. Various tools exist to help you to find information on the web:

1. *Catalog-style directories,* which are maintained by human editors who index web pages and reference them under categories that are offered to you on the screen, such as business, social sciences, or computers. The best known example of this type of web site is currently Yahoo!, These directories are useful if you are looking for information under a broad heading, such as distance learning, or resume services.. If you are interested in an area covered by one of the categories, this is a great way to begin

finding sites on the web. And each page that you visit may in turn refer you to other relevant sites.

2. *spider-based search engines,* are fed by automated spider programs that constantly patrol the web, indexing URL's and individual pages. Unlike the directories, they index every significant word of every page, allowing you to enter much more detailed searches. The first few lines, or a description of each page are shown on the screen, together with its URL, and if you want to go to that site, you just click on the underlined link. There are a number of these sites too.

Tips for using search tools

These tools vary widely in the number of pages they index, and the complexity of search criteria they allow. It is well worth trying the same query using several different engines, and comparing the results. If you are unsure of the timeliness of the web page that you retrieve, most of the major engines now include the date of the pages that they return. If not, your browser may allow you to view some information about the document.

Obstacles in searching

There are a few common problems that you may encounter:

1.Missing links

Web sites tend to change very frequently, and you may often encounter referrals to pages that no longer exist, or that no longer contain your search term. The spiders visit each page on an average of once a month, so they cannot be absolutely up to date at any time. If you think that the site you are looking for should still exist, try clicking into the Location box in your browser, and delete the last section of the URL (after the last /). Then press Enter. This will take you up a level to the referring page, and you may be able to follow the links it contains to find your subject.

2.Domain name not found

If you get this error, try clicking on the link again immediately. This particular domain name may not have been referenced by anyone before at your Internet provider, and is therefore not in their indexes, which is as far as their server looks on the first request. But if you request the domain a second time, their server will do a lookup beyond its own indexes.

3.Foreign languages

If the search engine gives you a page where the first few sentences seem to be in strange characters, that site is probably in a foreign language such as Japanese or Korean. Unless you have special software, your browser will not be able to display it.

Using bookmarks

Every web browser should contain a bookmark function. This allows you to record the URL of the page that you are currently visiting in your own personal directory with one click of the mouse. You can then return to that page later by calling up your bookmarks menu, and clicking on the name of the page that you wish to revisit.

Using master list sites

Because the web changes so much, it is a constant chore to ensure that all your bookmarks are current. Instead of trying to maintain your own exhaustive list of links around a particular subject, check for a master resource site that is updated by a reputable institution such as a library.

Printing and saving information from the web

Your browser should allow you to print out any web page currently on the screen. The command to do this will probably be found in a button on the toolbar, or under the File menu. However, remember that the printed page length will depend on your printer setup, and may not be exactly as it appears on the screen. You can also save web pages to your hard disk for subsequent use in a word processor, spreadsheet, or database.

Copyright issues

Much of the information that is available on the web is in the public domain - that is, free to be used by you after you download it. However, if you see a copyright notice you should certainly respect it. And if you are intending to quote someone, it is courteous to request their permission first-use the e-mail address given on the web page.

9

Doctrine in the Global Marketplace

This chapter aims to evaluate the validity of the 'fair use doctrine' in information society. To this end, a legal and economic aspect of the doctrine has been assessed to clarify whether the current international intellectual property system works for balanced economic and socio-cultural development in the global marketplace. Especially based on the economic characteristics and type of information goods, various specific criteria (such as specific classroom exemption, implied permission, interactive transmission rule, and market dynamics among players) are examined to figure out the appropriate level of protection for the copyrighted material across nations.

No one denies that intellectual products have been becoming an increasingly important component of national and international economies & socio-political development. That is, information and information-based products are not only valuable economic essentials in and of themselves: their use also increasingly affects the performance of other economic, and socio-cultural factors. It is very certain that information industry is becoming more and more important to the world economy and culture.

However, it is not rare to observe that only highly developed countries have earned profit from the development of electronic information markets. This is mainly because that developed countries are not only the producers of information but also effective users of information in fulfilling their economic and socio-cultural achievement. They are usually major owners and controllers for information distribution industry. Being an information rich country no longer means only the right of access to information but also the chance to produce, distribute and sell information. To the contrary, developing countries do not have sufficient manpower and information infrastructure for the efficient production and dissemination of information for their national development. In this vein, it might be inevitable and necessary to say that developing countries, rather than trying to produce their own but somewhat primitive information, would rather use of the information developed from other advanced countries as much as possible. However, while their dependence on imported information from the developed countries is getting increased, people in developing countries have to pay more than used to be just for the access to the information they want. In other words, as the degree of copyright protection in the global marketplace becomes higher and higher, accessing to wanted information becomes costly to many developing countries. It is not much surprised to see that people in developing countries are complaining of excessive copyright protection for the intellectual material in the global marketplace. Developing countries even argue that they are having hard time in developing their own information based on the copyrighted material of the advanced countries, due to severe restrictions and unduly expenses required for the access to the information. As a result, they believe that the gap between the developed and developing ones is widening rapidly in terms of information-handling capacity, losing the chance of balanced development across nations.

Various measures have been suggested to resolve the situation. A need for New World Information Order in the information society has been raised. Among them, international intellectual property system that seems to be mostly in favor of the copyright owners needs to be reexamined especially in terms of fair use doctrine, for the doctrine sometimes en facto provides useful defense mechanism against copyright infringement claims, leading to viable dissemination of information in the global marketplace.

Based on the rationale mentioned above, this chapter is designed to evaluate the validity of the 'fair use doctrine' as a way of assessing the appropriate level of protection for copyrighted material in the information society. To this end, a legal and economic aspect of the doctrine has been introduced to figure out whether current international intellectual property system works for balanced economic and socio-cultural development among nations, especially between the developed and developing ones. Integrated legal & economic viewpoint is useful to assess the validity of legal stipulation based on the analysis of its impact on marketability of copyrighted material. Cooter & Ulen (1988), in their book law and Economics, also support the usefulness of integrated perspective of economics and law in clarifying the validity of legal code. For the systematic study, this study will firstly investigate the nature and applicability of the fair use doctrine on the basis of type of copyrighted material flowing across nations. Then, several policy directions for the revision of international copyright system will be suggested especially in terms of applicability of fair use doctrine in the global marketplace.

Application of Fair Use Doctrine in the Global Marketplace

Before discussing about the fair use doctrine in the global marketplace, we need to realize that the copyright is not an inevitable right that confers on authors the absolute ownership of their creations. Rather it is designed to stimulate activity and progress in the arts and science for the intellectual enrichment of the public . Therefore, unlike patents, copyright law does not protect ideas, only their expression of the work in fixed form. The doctrine of fair use should be also understood in a direction to serve the nature of copyright mentioned above.

Until mid 20th century, the question of whether the defendant's conduct constituted a "fair use" was not clearly clarified at all for the conceptual ambiguity. The concept of "fair use" seems to be still dubious and not formulated at all. These days, interactive technologies' enormous power to copy, disseminate, manipulate electronic information makes even difficult to gauge the proper application of fair use in the marketplace. Leval (1990) argued that throughout the development of the fair use doctrine, courts has failed to fashion a set of governing principles or values. However, to certain point, it seems to be natural not to have any formula for fair use, for its judgment should be basically tailored to individual cases which may contain endless variety of situations. Having a standardized formula for fair use doctrine is not easy and even undesirable in terms of its legal flexibility in interpretation. Nonetheless, since Judge Story listed four factors for fair use judgment in Folsom v. Marsh, in 1841, the factors have been frequently cited in many cases. In approximate order of importance, the factors are : (1) impact on the potential market; (2) the purpose of uses; (3) the nature of copyrighted material at the time of the copying; and (4) amount of copying. In addition to the factors, customary practice without simple malice can be considered useful in determining whether copying of the copyrighted material without permission is within fair use domain or not.

The Court also identified four objectives that the doctrine of fair use ought to serve: (1) advancing social utility by increasing the supply of intellectual products and facilitating their distribution; (2) enforcing an author's natural right to a reasonable portion of the fruits of his labor; (3) protecting an author's interest in controlling the way in which his creations are presented to the world; and finally (4) aligning the law with custom and popular conceptions of decent behavior .

Several landmark court cases relating to the fair use doctrine have been made over time. They are: Folsom v. Marsh (1841) ; Basic Books, Inc. et al. v. Kinko's Graphics Corporation (1991) ; Princeton University Press v. Michigan document Services, Inc. (1992) ; Harper & Row, Publishers, Inc. v. Nation Enterprises (1985) ; Campbell v. Acuff-Rose Music, Inc. (1994) ; Frank Music Corporation v. CompuServe, Inc. (1995).

Deciding whether copying of intellectual material flowing across nations can be "fair use" should be also examined based on the considerations mentioned above. Besides, various types and characteristics of copyrighted material in the global marketplace need to be also analyzed to estimate if the current level of protection for the copyrighted material is appropriate. Basically the characteristics of intellectual material such as films and sound recordings flowed across nations can be defined as follows:

1) Nature/type of information: The nature of information is so important in deciding whether it is for fair use. As mentioned earlier, one of the functions of the fair use doctrine is to serve "advancing social utility" by increasing the supply of intellectual products. Accordingly if copying of information is for advancing social utility such as education or pure academic research for public interest, it is more likely to fall into the area of fair use than copying for commercial use. Types of information (entertainment/educational, commercial/non-commercial) is also useful to assess the appropriateness of fair use. In general, copying of information with substitutability is more likely to have a broader scope of fair use than information with monopolistic influence in the market. It seems to be necessary to empower the copyright owners to charge fees for the privilege of using information, and to acknowledge that mutually exclusive right of copyright holders for a certain period might cause monopoly losses, which vary between types of copyrighted material.

2) Characteristics of information goods: Information is basically public goods. Therefore it has the characteristics of non-excludability (in consumption)

and non-rivalry (in terms of utility). Accordingly copyright law forbidding users from unauthorized copying of intellectual products can be interpreted as a mechanism to eliminate the source of economic inefficiency by reviving excludability in information market. In a pay-per-use world, fair use rarely works, for pay-per-use could be carried to an extreme in which all electronic access and use require permission and/or payment . However, if information is sold to each individual, it becomes private goods though it still has a characteristic of non-rivalry. Information (whether it is educational or not) with competitive edge tends to have a lot of windows (or outlets) for consecutive sales of information. As the number of users increases, its LRAC (long range average cost) declines, too. It indicates that copying of the competitive information at the early stage could hamper its marketability seriously, leading to less possibility of fair use, unless the information lies in public domain.

A combination of information type & previously mentioned four factors for fair use allows us to have somewhat clear and predictable interpretation in deciding whether copying behavior without permission falls in the fair use domain as follows:

1) Information which is essential and useful for economic and socio-cultural development should have a broader area of fair use. Here the problem again lies in the conceptual ambiguity.

News: In general, foreign news is in nature very volatile and not much marketable for domestic news market, though it sometimes has significant socioeconomic and political value. Therefore its transmission with good customary standards of "good faith" is likely to fall in the area of fair use. Especially in the sense that the scope of fair use is generally broader when the source of borrowed expression is a factual or historical work, transmission of news deserves to enjoy broader fair use scope.

Movie film/sound recordings: Basically unauthorized copying of copyrighted movie film/sound can not be defensive at all. The scope of fair use is narrower with respect to unpublished works. Here, the productivity of copying itself should be carefully examined in the fair use calculus, for subordination of the idea of productivity is essential in facilitating the creation of derivative works.

Therefore, copying information without any value of economic or socio-cultural development is not likely to be in the public domain.

2) Information with competitive edge in general has a strong potential in making a lot of profit than one without competitive edge. As described earlier, the LRAC of information decreases as users of it increase. This implies the importance of timing of copying when deciding the proper scope of fair use. The nature of copyright is not to allow copyright owners to enjoy excessive economic fruit for their creativity, but to make favorable conditions for wider dissemination of information without seriously eroding the incentives for artistic and intellectual innovation. Therefore the unauthorized copying of unpublished intellectual materials is likely to hurt the property right of copyright owners seriously due to its impact on potential market of copyrighted material, while copying of already sufficiently consumed copyrighted material is likely to have a broader scope of fair use if it serves public interest.

News: Unauthorized copying of "hot" news has broader domain of fair use, for copying of unpublished news is in nature inexistent. Due to its volatility, copying of already known (disseminated) news does not pose any threat on the potential market of the news. Therefore, news traditionally enjoys the broader scope of fair use.

Movie film/sound recordings: Copying of unpublished movie film or sound recordings without seeking permission is fatal in their potential market, leaving no room for fair use. For example, when the movie film ET (Extra Terrestrial by Spielberg) was firstly introduced into Seoul several years ago, its illegal copy version had been already prevalent in Korea, leading to disastrous failure in the market. Copying of intellectual material for personal use also deserves the broader area of fair use, in that it does not usually pose serious threat on potential market of the material .

So far, we have discussed about several factors that can be considered in assessing the proper scope of fair use. Both characteristics of information goods and its role in society are scrutinized. The factors were in fact thoroughly examined in courts, whenever conflicts between copyright owners and copiers have been raised. Various rights granted to copyright owners are mostly resolved in market.

The problem still unresolved here is that various criteria for fair use, mentioned so far, are not much helpful in determining the optimal level of copyrighted protection. The key is to prevent copyright owners from collecting monopoly profits in greater than optimal amounts, allowing judges to use the fair use doctrine for the balanced interest among participants. It is necessary to develop various ways to reduce the gap between copyright holders' monopoly influence and users' desire to access the information. Standardized contract, compulsory licensing system, blanket licenses can be examined in domestic level, and revision of international copyright system in international level.

Basic Directions for the Revision of International Copyright System

Based on the analysis of criteria in assessing the scope of fair use, several policy suggestions for the appropriate level of copyrighted material in the global marketplace are made as follows:

1) The scope of fair use for advancing social utility (such as education, library copying, or creation of derivative work) should be enlarged even in digital society. Specifically specific classroom exemption should be respected even in the information society. Until now, some of the fair use guidelines for educational copying limit copying to a certain number of pages. These guidelines represent the minimum amount of copying which is considered as legal for educational purpose. Educational uses of music, digital image, et. al is not an infringement of copyright if the minimum amount of copying is made by the non-profit educational institution. For the educational purpose of digitized material, international copyright system should guarantee that non-profit educational institution may digitized newly, lawfully acquired analog visual images to support the permitted educational uses . However this exemption can be considered only in the situation where digitized products are not readily available in usable digital form for purchase or license at a fair price. Also so-called thumbnail

images of lawfully acquired images for educational or librarian purposes should be allowed to advance maximized social utilization of intellectual material. In case of derivative works, if they have minimum amount of originality, they can be acknowledged as legal. In other words, derivative works elaborated in developing countries, based on the originally copyrighted material, should be understood as fair use, in the sense that they could stimulate further development of creative works.

2) "Implied permission" needs to be widely reflected and implemented into the international copyright system. Implied permission has indeed played a role of exception against copyright infringement claims. For example, if copyright owners publicly display their information on the web, they allow users to use their information without permission, i.e., implied permission.

3) Recently the WCT (the WIPO Copyright Treaty) and the WPPT (WIPO Performances and Phonograms Treaty) include various provisions necessary for the adaptation of the international copyright norms. Especially some legal issues about interactive transmission need to be carefully examined when revising the framework of international copyright system in digital society. As the number of interactive media increases, a need for the right of public transmission has raised. This is mainly because that traditional definition of broadcasting or public performance has been diluted, though the definitions and rights of broadcasting and public performance have not changed for a long time in the international copyright system. The appropriate level of copyright protection for the material shown on interactive media needs to be reexamined.

4) Power dynamics among players in the market should be considered for deciding the appropriate level of copyright protection in international copyright system. For example, it is disclosed that performers in music industry in general do not enjoy economic benefits from the copyright law, for the law is designed to protect the right of information disseminators (such as TV or recording company), not for performers (such as musicians). This background lies in the EEC Rental Directive which was designed to prevent performers from being forced to agree to a buy-out of their rights. Nonetheless, excessive protection of neighboring rights of performers should be avoided for wide dissemination of information. Compulsory license and retransmission rule should be more actively utilized for the smoothing dissemination of information (which can be assumed as sufficiently consumed one in society) into developing countries. In sum, the application of the rules can be positively examined especially when the information serves for public interest.

5) Various international copyright systems such as the Berne Convention have changed over time to adjust themselves into new environment. As information society develops, copyright law will become more international than other areas of law. In this sense, international harmonization among countries is essential to avoid the conflict, and to fulfill the economic & socio-cultural achievement in global marketplace. Fair use doctrine, if well defined and articulated, could serve to deter the excessive protection of authors' rights to serve somewhat contradictory goals of copyright, i.e., wide dissemination of useful information & incentive for creative works.

Convention on Cybercrime

Explanatory Report (Adopted on 8 November 2001)

I. The Convention and its Explanatory Report have been adopted by the Committee of Ministers of the Council of Europe at its 109th Session (8 November 2001) and the Convention has been opened for signature in Budapest, on 23 November 2001, on the Issue of the International Conference on Cyber-crime.

II. The text of this explanatory report does not constitute an instrument providing an authoritative interpretation of the Convention, although it might be of such a nature as facilitate the application of the provisions contained therein.

I. Introduction

1. The revolution in information technologies has changed society fundamentally and will probably continue to do so in the foreseeable future. Many tasks have become easier to handle. Where originally

only some specific sectors of society had rationalised their working procedures with the help of information technology, now hardly any sector of society has remained unaffected. Information technology has in one way or the other pervaded almost every aspect of human activities.

2. A conspicuous feature of information technology is the impact it has had and will have on the evolution of telecommunications technology. Classical telephony, involving the transmission of human voice, has been overtaken by the exchange of vast amounts of data, comprising voice, text, music and static and moving pictures. This exchange no longer occurs only between human beings, but also between human beings and computers, and between computers themselves. Circuit-switched connections have been replaced by packet-switched networks. It is no longer relevant whether a direct connection can be established; it suffices that data is entered into a network with a destination address or made available for anyone who wants to access it.

3. The pervasive use of electronic mail and the accessing through the Internet of numerous web sites are examples of these developments. They have changed our society profoundly.

4. The ease of accessibility and searchability of information contained in computer systems, combined with the practically unlimited possibilities for its exchange and dissemination, regardless of geographical distances, has lead to an explosive growth in the amount of information available and the knowledge that can be drawn there from.

5. These developments have given rise to an unprecedented economic and social changes, but they also have a dark side: the emergence of new types of crime as well as the commission of traditional crimes by means of new technologies. Moreover, the consequences of criminal behaviour can be more far-reaching than before because they are not restricted by geographical limitations or national boundaries. The recent spread of detrimental computer viruses all over the world has provided proof of this reality. Technical measures to protect computer systems need to be implemented concomitantly with legal measures to prevent and deter criminal behaviour.

6. The new technologies challenge existing legal concepts. Information and communications flow more easily around the world. Borders are no longer boundaries to this flow. Criminals are increasingly located in places other than where their acts produce their effects. However, domestic laws are generally confined to a specific territory. Thus solutions to the problems posed must be addressed by international law, necessitating the adoption of adequate international legal instruments. The present Convention aims to meet this challenge, with due respect to human rights in the new Information Society.

II. The preparatory work

7. By decision CDPC/103/211196, the European Committee on Crime Problems (CDPC) decided in November 1996 to set up a committee of experts to deal with cyber-crime. The CDPC based its decision on the following rationale:

8. "The fast developments in the field of information technology have a direct bearing on all sections of modern society. The integration of telecommunication and information systems, enabling the storage and transmission, regardless of distance, of all kinds of communication opens a whole range of new possibilities. These developments were boosted by the emergence of information super-highways and networks, including the Internet, through which virtually anybody will be able to have access to any electronic information service irrespective of where in the world he is located. By connecting to communication and information services users create a kind of common space, called "cyber-space", which is used for legitimate purposes but may also be the subject of misuse. These "cyber-space offences" are either committed against the integrity, availability, and confidentiality of computer systems and telecommunication networks or they consist of the use of such networks of their services to commit traditional offences. The transborder character of such offences, e.g. when committed through the Internet, is in conflict with the territoriality of national law enforcement authorities.

9. The criminal law must therefore keep abreast of these technological developments which offer highly sophisticated opportunities for misusing facilities of the cyber-space and causing damage to legitimate interests. Given the cross-border nature of information networks, a concerted international effort is needed to deal with such misuse. Whilst Recommendation No. (89) 9 resulted in the approximation of national concepts regarding certain forms of computer misuse, only a binding

international instrument can ensure the necessary efficiency in the fight against these new phenomena. In the framework of such an instrument, in addition to measures of international co-operation, questions of substantive and procedural law, as well as matters that are closely connected with the use of information technology, should be addressed."

10. In addition, the CDPC took into account the Report, prepared - at its request - by Professor H.W.K. Kaspersen, which concluded that " ... it should be looked to another legal instrument with more engagement than a Recommendation, such as a Convention. Such a Convention should not only deal with criminal substantive law matters, but also with criminal procedural questions as well as with international criminal law procedures and agreements." (1) A similar conclusion emerged already from the Report attached to Recommendation N° R (89) 9 (2) concerning substantive law and from Recommendation N° R (95) 13 (3) concerning problems of procedural law connected with information technology.

II. The new committee's specific terms of reference were as follows:

i. "Examine, in the light of Recommendations No R (89) 9 on computer-related crime and No R (95) 13 concerning problems of criminal procedural law connected with information technology, in particular the following subjects:

ii. cyber-space offences, in particular those committed through the use of telecommunication networks, e.g. the Internet, such as illegal money transactions, offering illegal services, violation of copyright, as well as those which violate human dignity and the protection of minors;

iii. other substantive criminal law issues where a common approach may be necessary for the purposes of international co-operation such as definitions, sanctions and responsibility of the actors in cyber-space, including Internet service providers;

iv. the use, including the possibility of transborder use, and the applicability of coercive powers in a technological environment, e.g. interception of telecommunications and electronic surveillance of information networks, e.g. via the Internet, search and seizure in information-processing systems (including Internet sites), rendering illegal material inaccessible and requiring service providers to comply with special obligations, taking into account the problems caused by particular measures of information security, e.g. encryption;

v. the question of jurisdiction in relation to information technology offences, e.g. to determine the place where the offence was committed (locus delicti) and which law should accordingly apply, including the problem of ne bis idem in the case of multiple jurisdictions and the question how to solve positive jurisdiction conflicts and how to avoid negative jurisdiction conflicts;

vi. questions of international co-operation in the investigation of cyber-space offences, in close co-operation with the Committee of Experts on the Operation of European Conventions in the Penal Field (PC-OC).

The Committee should draft a binding legal instrument, as far as possible, on the items i) - v), with particular emphasis on international questions and, if appropriate, accessory recommendations regarding specific issues. The Committee may make suggestions on other issues in the light of technological developments."

12. Further to the CDPC's decision, the Committee of Ministers set up the new committee, called "the Committee of Experts on Crime in Cyber-space (PC-CY)" by decision n° CM/Del/Dec(97)583, taken at the 583rd meeting of the Ministers' Deputies (held on 4 February 1997). The Committee PC-CY started its work in April 1997 and undertook negotiations on a draft international convention on cyber-crime. Under its original terms of reference, the Committee was due to finish its work by 31 December 1999. Since by that time the Committee was not yet in a position to fully conclude its negotiations on certain issues in the draft Convention, its terms of reference were extended by decision n° CM/Del/Dec(99)679 of the Ministers' Deputies until 31 December 2000. The European Ministers of Justice expressed their support twice concerning the negotiations: by Resolution No. 1, adopted at their 21st Conference (Prague, June 1997), which recommended the Committee of Ministers to support the work carried out by the CDPC on cyber-crime in order to bring domestic criminal law provisions closer to each other and enable the use of effective means of investigation concerning such offences, as well as by Resolution N° 3, adopted at the 23rd Conference of the European Ministers of Justice (London, June 2000), which encouraged the negotiating parties to pursue their efforts with a view to finding appropriate solutions

so as to enable the largest possible number of States to become parties to the Convention and acknowledged the need for a swift and efficient system of international co-operation, which duly takes into account the specific requirements of the fight against cyber-crime. The member States of the European Union expressed their support to the work of the PC-CY through a Joint Position, adopted in May 1999.

13. Between April 1997 and December 2000, the Committee PC-CY held 10 meetings in plenary and 15 meetings of its open-ended Drafting Group. Following the expiry of its extended terms of reference, the experts held, under the aegis of the CDPC, three more meetings to finalise the draft Explanatory Memorandum and review the draft Convention in the light of the opinion of the Parliamentary Assembly. The Assembly was requested by the Committee of Ministers in October 2000 to give an opinion on the draft Convention, which it adopted at the 2nd part of its plenary session in April 2001.

14. Following a decision taken by the Committee PC-CY, an early version of the draft Convention was declassified and released in April 2000, followed by subsequent drafts released after each plenary meeting, in order to enable the negotiating States to consult with all interested parties. This consultation process proved useful.

15. The revised and finalised draft Convention and its Explanatory Memorandum were submitted for approval to the CDPC at its 50th plenary session in June 2001, following which the text of the draft

Convention was submitted to the Committee of Ministers for adoption and opening for signature.

III. The Convention

16. The Convention aims principally at (1) harmonising the domestic criminal substantive law elements of offences and connected provisions in the area of cyber-crime (2) providing for domestic criminal procedural law powers necessary for the investigation and prosecution of such offences as well as other offences committed by means of a computer system or evidence in relation to which is in electronic form (3) setting up a fast and effective regime of international co-operation.

17. The Convention, accordingly, contains four chapters: (I) Use of terms; (II) Measures to be taken at domestic level - substantive law and procedural law; (III) International co-operation; (IV) Final clauses.

18. Section 1 of Chapter II (substantive law issues) covers both criminalisation provisions and other connected provisions in the area of computer- or computer-related crime: it first defines 9 offences grouped in 4 different categories, then deals with ancillary liability and sanctions. The following offences are defined by the Convention: illegal access, illegal interception, data interference, system interference, misuse of devices, computer-related forgery, computer-related fraud, offences related to child pornography and offences related to copyright and neighbouring rights.

19. Section 2 of Chapter II (procedural law issues) - the scope of which goes beyond the offences defined in

Section 1 in that it applies to any offence committed by means of a computer system or the evidence of which is in electronic form – determines first the common conditions and safeguards, applicable to all procedural powers in this Chapter. It then sets out the following procedural powers: expedited preservation of stored data; expedited preservation and partial disclosure of traffic data; production order; search and seizure of computer data; real-time collection of traffic data; interception of content data. Chapter II ends with the jurisdiction provisions.

20. Chapter III contains the provisions concerning traditional and computer crime-related mutual assistance as well as extradition rules. It covers traditional mutual assistance in two situations: where no legal basis (treaty, reciprocal legislation, etc.) exists between parties – in which case its provisions apply – and where such a basis exists – in which case the existing arrangements also apply to assistance under this Convention. Computer- or computer-related crime specific assistance applies to both situations and covers, subject to extra-conditions, the same range of procedural powers as defined in Chapter II. In addition, Chapter III contains a provision on a specific type of transborder access to stored computer data which does not require mutual assistance (with consent or where publicly available) and provides for the setting up of a 24/7 network for ensuring speedy assistance among the Parties.

21. Finally, Chapter IV contains the final clauses, which - with certain exceptions - repeat the standard provisions in Council of Europe treaties.

COMMENTARY ON THE ARTICLES OF THE CONVENTION

Chapter I – Use of terms

Introduction to the definitions at Article 1

22. It was understood by the drafters that under this Convention Parties would not be obliged to copy verbatim into their domestic laws the four concepts defined in Article 1, provided that these laws cover such concepts in a manner consistent with the principles of the Convention and offer an equivalent framework for its implementation.

Article 1 (a) - Computer system

23. A computer system under the Convention is a device consisting of hardware and software developed for automatic processing of digital data. It may include input, output, and storage facilities. It may stand alone or be connected in a network with other similar devices "Automatic" means without direct human intervention, "processing of data" means that data in the computer system is operated by executing a computer program. A "computer program" is a set of instructions that can be executed by the computer to achieve the intended result. A computer can run different programs. A computer system usually consists of different devices, to be distinguished as the processor or central processing unit, and peripherals. A "peripheral" is a device that performs certain specific functions in interaction with the processing unit, such as a printer, video screen, CD reader/writer or other storage device.

24. A network is an interconnection between two or more computer systems. The connections may be earthbound (e.g., wire or cable), wireless (e.g., radio, infrared, or satellite), or both. A network may be geographically limited to a small area (local area networks) or may span a large area (wide area networks), and such networks may themselves be interconnected. The Internet is a global network consisting of many interconnected networks, all using the same protocols. Other types of networks exist, whether or not connected to the Internet, able to communicate computer data among computer systems. Computer systems may be connected to the network as endpoints or as a means to assist in communication on the network. What is essential is that data is exchanged over the network.

Article 1 (b) - Computer data

25. The definition of computer data builds upon the ISO-definition of data. This definition contains the terms "suitable for processing". This means that data is put in such a form that it can be directly processed by the computer system. In order to make clear that data in this Convention has to be understood as data in electronic or other directly processable form, the notion " computer data" is introduced. Computer data that is automatically processed may be the target of one of the criminal offences defined in this Convention as well as the object of the application of one of the investigative measures defined by this Convention.

Article 1 (c) - Service provider

26. The term "service provider" encompasses a broad category of persons that play a particular role with regard to communication or processing of data on computer systems (cf. also comments on Section 2). Under (i) of the definition, it is made clear that both public and private entities which provide users the ability to communicate with one another are covered. Therefore, it is irrelevant whether the users form a closed group or whether the provider offers its services to the public, whether free of charge or for a fee. The closed group can be e.g. the employees of a private enterprise to whom the service is offered by a corporate network.

27. Under (ii) of the definition, it is made clear that the term "service provider" also extends to those entities that store or otherwise process data on behalf of the persons mentioned under (i). Further, the term includes those entities that store or otherwise process data on behalf of the users of the services of those mentioned under (i). For example, under this definition, a service provider includes both services that provide hosting and caching services as well as services that provide a connection to a network. However, a mere provider of content (such as a person who contracts with a web hosting company to host his web site) is not intended to be covered by this definition if such content provider does not also offer communication or related data processing services.

Article 1 (d) - Traffic data

28. For the purposes of this Convention traffic data as

defined in article 1, under subparagraph d., is a category of computer data that is subject to a specific legal regime. This data is generated by computers in the chain of communication in order to route a communication from its origin to its destination. It is therefore auxiliary to the communication itself.

29. In case of an investigation of a criminal offence committed in relation to a computer system, traffic data is needed to trace the source of a communication as a starting point for collecting further evidence or as part of the evidence of the offence. Traffic data might last only ephemerally, which makes it necessary to order its expeditious preservation. Consequently, its rapid disclosure may be necessary to discern the communication's route in order to collect further evidence before it is deleted or to identify a suspect. The ordinary procedure for the collection and disclosure of computer data might therefore be insufficient. Moreover, the collection of this data is regarded in principle to be less intrusive since as such it doesn't reveal the content of the communication which is regarded to be more sensitive.

30. The definition lists exhaustively the categories of traffic data that are treated by a specific regime in this Convention: the origin of a communication, its destination, route, time (GMT), date, size, duration and type of underlying service. Not all of these categories will always be technically available, capable of being produced by a service provider, or necessary for a particular criminal investigation. The "origin" refers to a telephone number, Internet Protocol (IP) address, or similar identification of a communications facility to which a service provider

renders services. The "destination" refers to a comparable indication of a communications facility to which communications are transmitted. The term "type of underlying service" refers to the type of service that is being used within the network, e.g., file transfer, electronic mail, or instant messaging.

31. `The definition leaves to national legislatures the ability to introduce differentiation in the legal protection of traffic data in accordance with its sensitivity. In this context, Article 15 obliges the Parties to provide for conditions and safeguards that are adequate for protection of human rights and liberties. This implies, inter alia, that the substantive criteria and the procedure to apply an investigative power may vary according to the sensitivity of the data.

Chapter II – Measures to be taken at the national level

32. Chapter II (Articles 2 – 22) contains three sections: substantive criminal law (Articles 2 – 13), procedural law (Articles 14 – 21) and jurisdiction (Article 22).

Section 1 – Substantive criminal law

33. The purpose of Section 1 of the Convention (Articles 2 – 13) is to improve the means to prevent and suppress computer- or computer – related crime by establishing a common minimum standard of relevant offences. This kind of harmonisation alleviates the fight against such crimes on the national and on the international level as well. Correspondence in domestic law may prevent abuses from being shifted to a Party with a previous lower

standard. As a consequence, the exchange of useful common experiences in the practical handling of cases may be enhanced, too. International co-operation (esp. extradition and mutual legal assistance) is facilitated e.g. regarding requirements of double criminality.

34. The list of offences included represents a minimum consensus not excluding extensions in domestic law. To a great extent it is based on the guidelines developed in connection with Recommendation No. R (89) 9 of the Council of Europe on computer-related crime and on the work of other public and private international organisations (OECD, UN, AIDP), but taking into account more modern experiences with abuses of expanding telecommunication networks.

35. The section is divided into five titles. Title 1 includes the core of computer-related offences, offences against the confidentiality, integrity and availability of computer data and systems, representing the basic threats, as identified in the discussions on computer and data security to which electronic data processing and communicating systems are exposed. The heading describes the type of crimes which are covered, that is the unauthorised access to and illicit tampering with systems, programmes or data. Titles 2 – 4 include other types of 'computer-related offences', which play a greater role in practice and where computer and telecommunication systems are used as a means to attack certain legal interests which mostly are protected already by criminal law against attacks using traditional means. The Title 2 offences (computer-related fraud and forgery) have been added by following suggestions in the guidelines of the Council of Europe Recommendation No. R (89) 9.

Title 3 covers the 'content-related offences of unlawful production or distribution of child pornography by use of computer systems as one of the most dangerous modi operandi in recent times. The committee drafting the Convention discussed the possibility of including other content-related offences, such as the distribution of racist propaganda through computer systems. However, the committee was not in a position to reach consensus on the criminalisation of such conduct. While there was significant support in favour of including this as a criminal offence, some delegations expressed strong concern about including such a provision on freedom of expression grounds. Noting the complexity of the issue, it was decided that the committee would refer to the European Committee on Crime Problems (CDPC) the issue of drawing up an additional Protocol to the present Convention.

Title 4 sets out 'offences related to infringements of copyright and related rights'. This was included in the Convention because copyright infringements are one of the most widespread forms of computer- or computer-related crime and its escalation is causing international concern.

Finally, Title 5 includes additional provisions on attempt, aiding and abetting and sanctions and measures, and, in compliance with recent international instruments, on corporate liability.

36. Although the substantive law provisions relate to offences using information technology, the Convention uses technology-neutral language so that the substantive criminal law offences may be applied to both current and future technologies involved.

37. The drafters of the Convention understood that Parties may exclude petty or insignificant misconduct from implementation of the offences defined in Articles 2-10.

38. A specificity of the offences included is the express requirement that the conduct involved is done "without right". It reflects the insight that the conduct described is not always punishable per se, but may be legal or justified not only in cases where classical legal defences are applicable, like consent, self defence or necessity, but where other principles or interests lead to the exclusion of criminal liability. The expression 'without right' derives its meaning from the context in which it is used. Thus, without restricting how Parties may implement the concept in their domestic law, it may refer to conduct undertaken without authority (whether legislative, executive, administrative, judicial, contractual or consensual) or conduct that is otherwise not covered by established legal defences, excuses, justifications or relevant principles under domestic law. The Convention, therefore, leaves unaffected conduct undertaken pursuant to lawful government authority (for example, where the Party's government acts to maintain public order, protect national security or investigate criminal offences). Furthermore, legitimate and common activities inherent in the design of networks, or legitimate and common operating or commercial practices should not be criminalised. Specific examples of such exceptions from criminalisation are provided in relation to specific offences in the corresponding text of the Explanatory Memorandum below. It is left to the Parties to determine how such exemptions are

implemented within their domestic legal systems (under criminal law or otherwise).

39. All the offences contained in the Convention must be committed "intentionally" for criminal liability to apply. In certain cases an additional specific intentional element forms part of the offence. For instance, in Article 8 on computer-related fraud, the intent to procure an economic benefit is a constituent element of the offence. The drafters of the Convention agreed that the exact meaning of 'intentionally' should be left to national interpretation.

40. Certain articles in the section allow the addition of qualifying circumstances when implementing the Convention in domestic law. In other instances even the possibility of a reservation is granted (cf. Articles 40 and 42). These different ways of a more restrictive approach in criminalisation reflect different assessments of the dangerousness of the behaviour involved or of the need to use criminal law as a countermeasure. This approach provides flexibility to governments and parliaments in determining their criminal policy in this area.

41. Laws establishing these offences should be drafted with as much clarity and specificity as possible, in order to provide adequate foreseeability of the type of conduct that will result in a criminal sanction.

42. In the course of the drafting process, the drafters considered the advisability of criminalising conduct other than those defined at Articles 2 – 11, including the so-called cyber-squatting, i.e. the fact of registering a domain-name which is identical either to the name of an entity that already exists and is

usually well-known or to the trade-name or trademark of a product or company. Cyber-squatters have no intent to make an active use of the domain-name and seek to obtain a financial advantage by forcing the entity concerned, even though indirectly, to pay for the transfer of the ownership over the domain-name. At present this conduct is considered as a trademark-related issue. As trademark violations are not governed by this Convention, the drafters did not consider it appropriate to deal with the issue of criminalisation of such conduct.

Title 1 - Offences against the confidentiality, integrity and availability of computer data and systems

43. The criminal offences defined under (Articles 2-6) are intended to protect the confidentiality, integrity and availability of computer systems or data and not to criminalise legitimate and common activities inherent in the design of networks, or legitimate and common operating or commercial practices.

Illegal access (Article 2)

44. "Illegal access" covers the basic offence of dangerous threats to and attacks against the security (i.e. the confidentiality, integrity and availability) of computer systems and data. The need for protection reflects the interests of organisations and individuals to manage, operate and control their systems in an undisturbed and uninhibited manner. The mere unauthorised intrusion, i.e. "hacking", "cracking" or "computer trespass" should in principle be illegal in itself. It may lead to impediments to legitimate users of systems and data and may cause alteration or destruction

with high costs for reconstruction. Such intrusions may give access to confidential data (including passwords, information about the targ~ted system) and secrets, to the use of the system without payment or even encourage hackers to commit more dangerous forms of computer-related offences, like computer-related fraud or forgery

45. The most effective means of preventing unauthorised access is, of course, the introduction and development of effective security measures. However, a comprehensive response has to include also the threat and use of criminal law measures. A criminal prohibition of unauthorised access is able to give additional protection to the system and the data as such and at an early stage against the dangers described above.

46. "Access" comprises the entering of the whole or any part of a computer system (hardware, components, stored data of the system installed, directories, traffic and content-related data). However, it does not include the mere sending of an e-mail message or file to that system. "Access" includes the entering of another computer system, where it is connected via public telecommunication networks, or to a computer system on the same network, such as a LAN (local area network) or Intranet within an organisation. The method of communication (e.g. from a distance, including via wireless links or at a close range) does not matter.

47. The act must also be committed 'without right'. In addition to the explanation given above on this expression, it means that there is no criminalisation of the access authorised by the owner or other right

holder of the system or part of it (such as for the purpose of authorised testing or protection of the computer system concerned). Moreover, there is no criminalisation for accessing a computer system that permits free and open access by the public, as such access is "with right."

48. The application of specific technical tools may result in an access under Article 2, such as the access of a web page, directly or through hypertext links, including deep-links or the application of 'cookies' or 'bots' to locate and retrieve information on behalf of communication. The application of such tools per se is not 'without right'. The maintenance of a public web site implies consent by the web site-owner that it can be accessed by any other web-user. The application of standard tools provided for in the commonly applied communication protocols and programs, is not in itself 'without right', in particular where the rightholder of the accessed system can be considered to have accepted its application, e.g. in the case of 'cookies' by not rejecting the initial instalment or not removing it.

49. Many national legislations already contain provisions on "hacking" offences, but the scope and constituent elements vary considerably. The broad approach of criminalisation in the first sentence of Article 2 is not undisputed. Opposition stems from situations where no dangers were created by the mere intrusion or where even acts of hacking have led to the detection of loopholes and weaknesses of the security of systems. This has led in a range of countries to a narrower approach requiring additional qualifying circumstances which is also the approach adopted by

Recommendation N° (89) 9 and the proposal of the OECD Working Party in 1985.

50. Parties can take the wide approach and criminalise mere hacking in accordance with the first sentence of Article 2. Alternatively, Parties can attach any or all of the qualifying elements listed in the second sentence: infringing security measures, special intent to obtain computer data, other dishonest intent that justifies criminal culpability, or the requirement that the offence is committed in relation to a computer system that is connected remotely to another computer system. The last option allows Parties to exclude the situation where a person physically accesses a stand-alone computer without any use of another computer system. They may restrict the offence to illegal access to networked computer systems (including public networks provided by telecommunication services and private networks, such as Intranets or Extranets).

Illegal interception (Article 3)

51. This provision aims to protect the right of privacy of data communication. The offence represents the same violation of the privacy of communications as traditional tapping and recording of oral telephone conversations between persons. The right to privacy of correspondence is enshrined in Article 8 of the European Convention on Human Rights. The offence established under Article 3 applies this principle to all forms of electronic data transfer, whether by telephone, fax, e-mail or file transfer.

52. The text of the provision has been mainly taken from the offence of 'unauthorised interception' contained in Recommendation (89) 9. In the present Convention it has been made clear that the communications involved concern "transmissions of computer data" as well as electromagnetic radiation, under the circumstances as explained below.

53. Interception by 'technical means' relates to listening to, monitoring or surveillance of the content of communications, to the procuring of the content of data either directly, through access and use of the computer system, or indirectly, through the use of electronic eavesdropping or tapping devices. Interception may also involve recording. Technical means includes technical devices fixed to transmission lines as well as devices to collect and record wireless communications. They may include the use of software, passwords and codes. The requirement of using technical means is a restrictive qualification to avoid over-criminalisation.

54. The offence applies to 'non-public' transmissions of computer data. The term 'non-public' qualifies the nature of the transmission (communication) process and not the nature of the data transmitted. The data communicated may be publicly available information, but the parties wish to communicate confidentially. Or data may be kept secret for commercial purposes until the service is paid, as in Pay-TV. Therefore, the term 'non-public' does not per se exclude communications via public networks. Communications of employees, whether or not for business purposes, which constitute "non-public transmissions of computer data" are also protected against interception without right under Article.).

55. The communication in the form of transmission of computer data can take place inside a single computer system (flowing from CPU to screen or printer, for example), between two computer systems belonging to the same person, two computers communicating with one another, or a computer and a person (e.g. through the keyboard). Nonetheless, Parties may require as an additional element that the communication be transmitted between computer systems remotely connected.

56. It should be noted that the fact that the notion of 'computer system' may also encompass radio connections does not mean that a Party is under an obligation to criminalise the interception of any radio transmission which, even though 'non-public', takes place in a relatively open and easily accessible manner and therefore can be intercepted, for example by radio amateurs.

57. The creation of an offence in relation to 'electromagnetic emissions' will ensure a more comprehensive scope. Electromagnetic emissions may be emitted by a computer during its operation. Such emissions are not considered as 'data' according to the definition provided in Article 1. However, data can be reconstructed from such emissions. Therefore, the interception of data from electromagnetic emissions from a computer system is included as an offence under this provision.

58. For criminal liability to attach, the illegal interception must be committed "intentionally", and "without right". The act is justified, for example, if the intercepting person has the right to do so, if he acts on the instructions or by authorisation of the

participants of the transmission (including authorised testing or protection activities agreed to by the participants), or if surveillance is lawfully authorised in the interests of national security or the detection of offences by investigating authorities. It was also understood that the use of common commercial practices, such as employing 'cookies', is not intended to be criminalised as such, as not being an interception "without right". With respect to non-public communications of employees protected under Article 3 domestic law may provide a ground for legitimate interception of such communications. Under Article 3, interception in such circumstances would be considered as undertaken "with right".

59. In some countries, interception may be closely related to the offence of unauthorised access to a computer system. In order to ensure consistency of the prohibition and application of the law, countries that require dishonest intent, or that the offence be committed in relation to a computer system that is connected to another computer system in accordance with Article 2, may also require similar qualifying elements to attach criminal liability in this article. These elements should be interpreted and applied in conjunction with the other elements of the offence, such as "intentionally" and "without right".

Data interference (Article 4)

60. The aim of this provision is to provide computer data and computer programs with protection similar to that enjoyed by corporeal objects against intentional infliction of damage. The protected legal interest here

is the integrity and the proper functioning or use of stored computer data or computer programs.

61. In paragraph 1, 'damaging' and 'deteriorating' as overlapping acts relate in particular to a negative alteration of the integrity or of information content of data and programmes. 'Deletion' of data is the equivalent of the destruction of a corporeal thing. It destroys them and makes them unrecognisable. Suppressing of computer data means any action that prevents or terminates the availability of the data to the person who has access to the computer or the data carrier on which it was stored. The term 'alteration' means the modification of existing data. The input of malicious codes, such as viruses and Trojan horses is, therefore, covered under this paragraph, as is the resulting modification of the data.

62. The above acts are only punishable if committed "without right". Common activities inherent in the design of networks or common operating or commercial practices, such as, for example, for the testing or protection of the security of a computer system authorised by the owner or operator, or the reconfiguration of a computer's operating system that takes place when the operator of a system acquires new software (e.g., software permitting access to the Internet that disables similar, previously installed programs), are with right and therefore are not criminalised by this article. The modification of traffic data for the purpose of facilitating anonymous communications (e.g., the activities of anonymous remailer systems), or the modification of data for the purpose of secure communications (e.g. encryption),

should in principle be considered a legitimate protection of privacy and, therefore, be considered as being undertaken with right. However, Parties may wish to criminalise certain abuses related to anonymous communications, such as where the packet header information is altered in order to conceal the identity of the perpetrator in committing a crime.

63. In addition, the offender must have acted "intentionally".

64. Paragraph 2 allows Parties to enter a reservation concerning the offence in that they may require that the conduct result in serious harm. The interpretation of what constitutes such serious harm is left to domestic legislation, but Parties should notify the Secretary General of the Council of Europe of their interpretation if use is made of this reservation possibility.

System interference (Article 5)

65. This is referred to in Recommendation No. (89) 9 as computer sabotage. The provision aims at criminalising the intentional hindering of the lawful use of computer systems including telecommunications facilities by using or influencing computer data. The protected legal interest is the interest of operators and users of computer or telecommunication systems being able to have them function properly. The text is formulated in a neutral way so that all kinds of functions can be protected by it.

66. The term "hindering" refers to actions that interfere

with the proper functioning of the computer system. Such hindering must take place by inputting, transmitting, damaging, deleting, altering or suppressing computer data.

67. The hindering must furthermore be "serious" in order to give rise to criminal sanction. Each Party shall determine for itself what criteria must be fulfilled in order for the hindering to be considered "serious." For example, a Party may require a minimum amount of damage to be caused in order for the hindering to be considered serious. The drafters considered as "serious" the sending of data to a particular system in such a form, size or frequency that it has a significant detrimental effect on the ability of the owner or operator to use the system, or to communicate with other systems (e.g., by means of programs that generate "denial of service" attacks, malicious codes such as viruses that prevent or substantially slow the operation of the system, or programs that send huge quantities of electronic mail to a recipient in order to block the communications functions of the system).

68. The hindering must be "without right". Common activities inherent in the design of networks, or common operational or commercial practices are with right. These include, for example, the testing of the security of a computer system, or its protection, authorised by its owner or operator, or the reconfiguration of a computer's operating system that takes place when the operator of a system installs new software that disables similar, previously installed programs. Therefore, such conduct is not criminalised by this article, even if it causes serious

hindering.

69. The sending of unsolicited e-mail, for commercial or other purposes, may cause nuisance to its recipient, in particular when such messages are sent in large quantities or with a high frequency ("spamming"). In the opinion of the drafters, such conduct should only be criminalised where the communication is intentionally and seriously hindered. Nevertheless, Parties may have a different approach to hindrance under their law, e.g. by making particular acts of interference administrative offences or otherwise subject to sanction. The text leaves it to the Parties to determine the extent to which the functioning of the system should be hindered – partially or totally, temporarily or permanently – to reach the threshold of harm that justifies sanction, administrative or criminal, under their law.

70. The offence must be committed intentionally, that is the perpetrator must have the intent to seriously hinder.

Misuse of devices (Article 6)

71. This provision establishes as a separate and independent criminal offence the intentional commission of specific illegal acts regarding certain devices or access data to be misused for the purpose of committing the above-described offences against the confidentiality, the integrity and availability of computer systems or data. As the commission of these offences often requires the possession of means of access ("hacker tools") or other tools, there is a strong incentive to acquire them for criminal

purposes which may then lead to the creation of a kind of black market in their production and distribution. To combat such dangers more effectively, the criminal law should prohibit specific potentially dangerous acts at the source, preceding the commission of offences under Articles 2 – 5. In this respect the provision builds upon recent developments inside the Council of Europe (European Convention on the legal protection of services based on, or consisting of, conditional access - ETS N° 178) and the European Union (Directive 98/84/EC of the European Parliament and of the Council of 20 November 1998 on the legal protection of services based on, or consisting of, conditional access) and relevant provisions in some countries. A similar approach has already been taken in the 1929 Geneva Convention on currency counterfeiting.

72. Paragraph 1(a)1 criminalises the production, sale, procurement for use, import, distribution or otherwise making available of a device, including a computer programme, designed or adapted primarily for the purpose of committing any of the offences established in Articles 2-5 of the present Convention. 'Distribution' refers to the active act of forwarding data to others, while 'making available' refers to the placing online devices for the use of others. This term also intends to cover the creation or compilation of hyperlinks in order to facilitate access to such devices. The inclusion of a 'computer program' refers to programs that are for example designed to alter or even destroy data or interfere with the operation of systems, such as virus programs, or programs designed or adapted to gain access to computer systems.

73. The drafters debated at length whether the devices should be restricted to those which are designed exclusively or specifically for committing offences, thereby excluding dual-use devices. This was considered to be too narrow. It could lead to insurmountable difficulties of proof in criminal proceedings, rendering the provision practically inapplicable or only applicable in rare instances. The alternative to include all devices even if they are legally produced and distributed, was also rejected. Only the subjective element of the intent of committing a computer offence would then be decisive for imposing a punishment, an approach which in the area of money counterfeiting also has not been adopted. As a reasonable compromise the Convention restricts its scope to cases where the devices are objectively designed, or adapted, primarily for the purpose of committing an offence. This alone will usually exclude dual-use devices.

74. Paragraph 1(a)2 criminalises the production, sale, procurement for use, import, distribution or otherwise making available of a computer password, access code or similar data by which the whole or any part of a computer system is capable of being accessed.

75. Paragraph 1(b) creates the offence of possessing the items set out in paragraph 1(a)1 or 1(a)2. Parties are permitted, by the last phrase of paragraph 1(b), to require by law that a number of such items be possessed. The number of items possessed goes directly to proving criminal intent. It is up to each Party to decide the number of items required before criminal liability attaches.

76. The offence requires that it be committed intentionally and without right. In order to avoid the danger of overcriminalisation where devices are produced and put on the market for legitimate purposes, e.g. to counter-attacks against computer systems, further elements are added to restrict the offence. Apart from the general intent requirement, there must be the specific (i.e. direct) intent that the device is used for the purpose of committing any of the offences established in Articles 2-5 of the Convention.

77. Paragraph 2 sets out clearly that those tools created for the authorised testing or the protection of a computer system are not covered by the provision. This concept is already contained in the expression 'without right'. For example, test-devices ('cracking-devices') and network analysis devices designed by industry to control the reliability of their information technology products or to test system security are produced for legitimate purposes, and would be considered to be 'with right'.

78. Due to different assessments of the need to apply the offence of "Misuse of Devices" to all of the different kinds of computer offences in Articles 2 – 5, paragraph 3 allows, on the basis of a reservation (cf. Article 42), to restrict the offence in domestic law. Each Party is, however, obliged to criminalise at least the sale, distribution or making available of a computer password or access data as described in paragraph 1 (a) 2.

Title 2 - Computer-related offences

79. Articles 7 - 10 relate to ordinary crimes that are frequently committed through the use of a computer

system. Most States already have criminalised these ordinary crimes, and their existing laws may or may not be sufficiently broad to extend to situations involving computer networks (for example, existing child pornography laws of some States may not extend to electronic images). Therefore, in the course of implementing these articles, States must examine their existing laws to determine whether they apply to situations in which computer systems or networks are involved. If existing offences already cover such conduct, there is no requirement to amend existing offences or enact new ones.

80. "Computer-related forgery" and "Computer-related fraud" deal with certain computer-related offences, i.e. computer-related forgery and computer-related fraud as two specific kinds of manipulation of computer systems or computer data. Their inclusion acknowledges the fact that in many countries certain traditional legal interests are not sufficiently protected against new forms of interference and attacks.

Computer-related forgery (Article 7)

81. The purpose of this article is to create a parallel offence to the forgery of tangible documents. It aims at filling gaps in criminal law related to traditional forgery, which requires visual readability of statements, or declarations embodied in a document and which does not apply to electronically stored data. Manipulations of such data with evidentiary value may have the same serious consequences as traditional acts of forgery if a third party is thereby

misled. Computer-related forgery involves unauthorised creating or altering stored data so that they acquire a different evidentiary value in the course of legal transactions, which relies on the authenticity of information contained in the data, is subject to a deception. The protected legal interest is the security and reliability of electronic data which may have consequences for legal relations.

82. It should be noted that national concepts of forgery vary greatly. One concept is based on the authenticity as to the author of the document, and others are based on the truthfulness of the statement contained in the document. However, it was agreed that the deception as to authenticity refers at minimum to the issuer of the data, regardless of the correctness or veracity of the contents of the data. Parties may go further and include under the term "authentic" the genuineness of the data.

83. This provision covers data which is the equivalent of a public or private document, which has legal effects. The unauthorised "input" of correct or incorrect data brings about a situation that corresponds to the making of a false document. Subsequent alterations (modifications, variations, partial changes), deletions (removal of data from a data medium) and suppression (holding back, concealment of data) correspond in general to the falsification of a genuine document.

84. The term "for legal purposes" refers also to legal transactions and documents which are legally relevant.

85. The final sentence of the provision allows Parties, when implementing the offence in domestic law, to

require in addition an intent to defraud, or similar dishonest intent, before criminal liability attaches.

Computer-related fraud (Article 8)

86. With the arrival of the technological revolution the opportunities for committing economic crimes such as fraud, including credit card fraud, have multiplied. Assets represented or administered in computer systems (electronic funds, deposit money) have become the target of manipulations like traditional forms of property. These crimes consist mainly of input manipulations, where incorrect data is fed into the computer, or by programme manipulations and other interferences with the course of data processing. The aim of this article is to criminalise any undue manipulation in the course of data processing with the intention to effect an illegal transfer of property.

87. To ensure that all possible relevant manipulations are covered, the constituent elements of 'input', 'alteration', 'deletion' or 'suppression' in Article 8(a) are supplemented by the general act of 'interference with the functioning of a computer programme or system' in Article 8(b). The elements of 'input, alteration, deletion or suppression' have the same meaning as in the previous articles. Article 8(b) covers acts such as hardware manipulations, acts suppressing printouts and acts affecting recording or flow of data, or the sequence in which programs are run.

88. The computer fraud manipulations are criminalised if they produce a direct economic or possessory loss of

another person's property and the perpetrator acted with the intent of procuring an unlawful economic gain for himself or for another person. The term 'loss of property', being a broad notion, includes loss of money, tangibles and intangibles with an economic value.

89. The offence must be committed "without right", and the economic benefit must be obtained without right. Of course, legitimate common commercial practices, which are intended to procure an economic benefit, are not meant to be included in the offence established by this article because they are conducted with right. For example, activities carried out pursuant to a valid contract between the affected persons are with right (e.g. disabling a web site as entitled pursuant to the terms of the contract).

90. The offence has to be committed "intentionally". The general intent element refers to the computer manipulation or interference causing loss of property to another. The offence also requires a specific fraudulent or other dishonest intent to gain an economic or other benefit for oneself or another. Thus, for example, commercial practices with respect to market competition that may cause an economic detriment to a person and benefit to another, but are not carried out with fraudulent or dishonest intent, are not meant to be included in the offence established by this article. For example, the use of information gathering programs to comparison shop on the Internet ("bots"), even if not authorised by a site visited by the "bot" is not intended to be criminalised.

Title 3 – Content-related offences

Offences related to child pornography (Article 9)

91. Article 9 on child pornography seeks to strengthen protective measures for children, including their protection against sexual exploitation, by modernising criminal law provisions to more effectively circumscribe the use of computer systems in the commission of sexual offences against children.

92. This provision responds to the preoccupation of Heads of State and Government of the Council of Europe, expressed at their 2nd summit (Strasbourg, 10 - 11 October 1997) in their Action Plan (item III.4) and corresponds to an international trend that seeks to ban child pornography, as evidenced by the recent adoption of the Optional Protocol to the UN Convention on the rights of the child, on the sale of children, child prostitution and child pornography and the recent European Commission initiative on combating sexual exploitation of children and child pornography (COM2000/854).

93. This provision criminalises various aspects of the electronic production, possession and distribution of child pornography. Most States already criminalise the traditional production and physical distribution of child pornography, but with the ever-increasing use of the Internet as the primary instrument for trading such material, it was strongly felt that specific provisions in an international legal instrument were essential to combat this new form of sexual exploitation and endangerment of children. It is widely believed that such material and on-line

practices, such as the exchange of ideas, fantasies and advice among paedophiles, play a role in supporting, encouraging or facilitating sexual offences against children.

94. Paragraph 1(a) criminalises the production of child pornography for the purpose of distribution through a computer system. This provision was felt necessary to combat the dangers described above at their source.

95. Paragraph 1(b) criminalises the 'offering' of child pornography through a computer system. 'Offering' is intended to cover soliciting others to obtain child pornography. It implies that the person offering the material can actually provide it. 'Making available' is intended to cover the placing of child pornography on line for the use of others e.g. by means of creating child pornography sites. This paragraph also intends to cover the creation or compilation of hyperlinks to child pornography sites in order to facilitate access to child pornography.

96. Paragraph 1(c) criminalises the distribution or transmission of child pornography through a computer system. 'Distribution' is the active dissemination of the material. Sending child pornography through a computer system to another person would be addressed by the offence of 'transmitting' child pornography.

97. The term 'procuring for oneself or for another' in paragraph 1(d) means actively obtaining child pornography, e.g. by downloading it.

98. The possession of child pornography in a computer system or on a data carrier, such as a diskette or CD-

Rom, is criminalised in paragraph 1(e). The possession of child pornography stimulates demand for such material. An effective way to curtail the production of child pornography is to attach criminal consequences to the conduct of each participant in the chain from production to possession.

99. The term 'pornographic material' in paragraph 2 is governed by national standards pertaining to the classification of materials as obscene, inconsistent with public morals or similarly corrupt. Therefore, material having an artistic, medical, scientific or similar merit may be considered not to be pornographic. The visual depiction includes data stored on computer diskette or on other electronic means of storage, which are capable of conversion into a visual image.

100. A 'sexually explicit conduct' covers at least real or simulated: a) sexual intercourse, including genital-genital, oral-genital, anal-genital or oral-anal, between minors, or between an adult and a minor, of the same or opposite sex; b) bestiality; c) masturbation; d) sadistic or masochistic abuse in a sexual context; or e) lascivious exhibition of the genitals or the pubic area of a minor. It is not relevant whether the conduct depicted is real or simulated.

101. The three types of material defined in paragraph 2 for the purposes of committing the offences contained in paragraph 1 cover depictions of sexual abuse of a real child (2a), pornographic images which depict a person appearing to be a minor engaged in sexually explicit conduct (2b), and finally images, which, although 'realistic', do not in fact involve a

real child engaged in sexually explicit conduct (2c). This latter scenario includes pictures which are altered, such as morphed images of natural persons, or even generated entirely by the computer.

102. In the three cases covered by paragraph 2, the protected legal interests are slightly different. Paragraph 2(a) focuses more directly on the protection against child abuse. Paragraphs 2(b) and 2(c) aim at providing protection against behaviour that, while not necessarily creating harm to the 'child' depicted in the material, as there might not be a real child, might be used to encourage or seduce children into participating in such acts, and hence form part of a subculture favouring child abuse.

103. The term 'without right' does not exclude legal defences, excuses or similar relevant principles that relieve a person of responsibility under specific circumstances. Accordingly, the term 'without right' allows a Party to take into account fundamental rights, such as freedom of thought, expression and privacy. In addition, a Party may provide a defence in respect of conduct related to "pornographic material" having an artistic, medical, scientific or similar merit. In relation to paragraph 2(b), the reference to 'without right' could also allow, for example, that a Party may provide that a person is relieved of criminal responsibility if it is established that the person depicted is not a minor in the sense of this provision.

104. Paragraph 3 defines the term 'minor' in relation to child pornography in general as all persons under 18 years, in accordance with the definition of a 'child' in the UN Convention on the Rights of the Child

(Article 1). It was considered an important policy matter to set a uniform international standard regarding age. It should be noted that the age refers to the use of (real or fictitious) children as sexual objects, and is separate from the age of consent for sexual relations.

Nevertheless, recognising that certain States require a lower age-limit in national legislation regarding child pornography, the last phrase of paragraph 3 allows Parties to require a different age-limit, provided it is not less than 16 years.

105. This article lists different types of illicit acts related to child pornography which, as in articles 2 - 8, Parties are obligated to criminalise if committed "intentionally." Under this standard, a person is not liable unless he has an intent to offer, make available, distribute, transmit, produce or possess child pornography. Parties may adopt a more specific standard (see, for example, applicable European Community law in relation to service provider liability), in which case that standard would govern. For example, liability may be imposed if there is "knowledge and control" over the information which is transmitted or stored. It is not sufficient, for example, that a service provider served as a conduit for, or hosted a website or newsroom containing such material, without the required intent under domestic law in the particular case. Moreover, a service provider is not required to monitor conduct to avoid criminal liability.

106. Paragraph 4 permits Parties to make reservations regarding paragraph 1(d) and (e), and paragraph 2(b) and (c). The right not to apply these sections of the

provision may be made in part or in whole. Any such reservation should be declared to the Secretary General of the Council of Europe at the time of signature or when depositing the Party's instruments of ratification, acceptance, approval or accession, in accordance with Article 42.

Title 4 - Offences related to infringements of copyright and related rights

Offences related to infringements of copyright and related rights (Article 10)

107. Infringements of intellectual property rights, in particular of copyright, are among the most commonly committed offences on the Internet, which cause concern both to copyright holders and those who work professionally with computer networks. The reproduction and dissemination on the Internet of protected works, without the approval of the copyright holder, are extremely frequent. Such protected works include literary, photographic, musical, audio-visual and other works. The ease with which unauthorised copies may be made due to digital technology and the scale of reproduction and dissemination in the context of electronic networks made it necessary to include provisions on criminal law sanctions and enhance international co-operation in this field.

108. Each Party is obliged to criminalise wilful infringements of copyright and related rights, sometimes referred to as neighbouring rights, arising from the agreements listed in the article, when such infringements have been committed by means of a

computer system and on a commercial scale". Paragraph 1 provides for criminal sanctions against infringements of copyright by means of a computer system. Infringement of copyright is already an offence in almost all States. Paragraph 2 deals with the infringement of related rights by means of a computer system.

109. Infringement of both copyright and related rights is as defined under the law of each Party and pursuant to the obligations the Party has undertaken in respect of certain international instruments. While each Party is required to establish as criminal offences those infringements, the precise manner in which such infringements are defined under domestic law may vary from State to State. However, criminalisation obligations under the Convention do not cover intellectual property infringements other that those explictly addressed in Article 10 and thus exclude patent or trademark-related violations.

110. With regard to paragraph 1, the agreements referred to are the Paris Act of 24 July 1971 of the Bern Convention for the Protection of Literary and Artistic Works, the Agreement on Trade-Related Aspects of Intellectual Property Rights (TRIPS), and the World Intellectual Property Organisation (WIPO) Copyright Treaty. With regard to paragraph 2, the international instruments cited are the International Convention for the Protection of Performers, Producers of Phonograms and Broadcasting Organisations (Rome Convention), the Agreement on Trade-Related Aspects of Intellectual Property Rights (TRIPS) and the World Intellectual Property Organisation (WIPO) Performances and Phonograms Treaty. The use of the

term "pursuant to the obligations it has undertaken" in both paragraphs makes it clear that a Contracting Party to the current Convention is not bound to apply agreements cited to which it is not a Party; moreover, if a Party has made a reservation or declaration permitted under one of the agreements, that reservation may limit the extent of its obligation under the present Convention.

111. The WIPO Copyright Treaty and the WIPO Performances and Phonograms Treaty had not entered into force at the time of concluding the present Convention. These treaties are nevertheless important as they significantly update the international protection for intellectual property (especially with regard to the new right of 'making available' of protected material 'on demand' over the Internet) and improve the means to fight violations of intellectual property rights worldwide. However it is understood that the infringements of rights established by these treaties need not be criminalised under the present Convention until these treaties have entered into force with respect to a Party.

112. The obligation to criminalise infringements of copyright and related rights pursuant to obligations undertaken in international instruments does not extend to any moral rights conferred by the named instruments (such as in Article 6bis of the Bern Convention and in Article 5 of the WIPO Copyright Treaty).

113. Copyright and related rights offences must be committed "wilfully" for criminal liability to apply. In contrast to all the other substantive law provisions of this Convention, the term "wilfully" is used instead of

"intentionally" in both paragraphs 1 and 2, as this is the term employed in the TRIPS Agreement (Article 61), governing the obligation to criminalise copyright violations.

114. The provisions are intended to provide for criminal sanctions against infringements 'on a commercial scale' and by means of a computer system. This is in line with Article 61 of the TRIPS Agreement which requires criminal sanctions in copyright matters only in the case of "piracy on a commercial scale". However, Parties may wish to go beyond the threshold of "commercial scale" and criminalise other types of copyright infringement as well.

115. The term "without right" has been omitted from the text of this article as redundant, since the term "infringement" already denotes use of the copyrighted material without authorisation. The absence of the term "without right" does not a contrario exclude application of criminal law defences, justifications and principles governing the exclusion of criminal liability associated with the term "without right" elsewhere in the Convention.

116. Paragraph 3 allows Parties not to impose criminal liability under paragraphs 1 and 2 in "limited circumstances" (e.g. parallel imports, rental rights), as long as other effective remedies, including civil and/ or administrative measures, are available. This provision essentially allows Parties a limited exemption from the obligation to impose criminal liability, provided that they do not derogate from obligations under Article 61 of the TRIPS Agreement, which is the minimum pre-existing criminalisation requirement.

117. This article shall in no way be interpreted to extend the protection granted to authors, film producers, performers, producers of phonograms, broadcasting organisations or other right holders to persons that do not meet the criteria for eligibility under domestic law or international agreement.

Title 5 - Ancillary liability and sanctions

Attempt and aiding or abetting (Article 11)

118. The purpose of this article is to establish additional offences related to attempt and aiding or abetting the commission of the offences defined in the Convention. As discussed further below, it is not required that a Party criminalise the attempt to commit each offence established in the Convention.

119. Paragraph 1 requires Parties to establish as criminal offences aiding or abetting the commission of any of the offences under Articles 2-10. Liability arises for aiding or abetting where the person who commits a crime established in the Convention is aided by another person who also intends that the crime be committed. For example, although the transmission of harmful content data or malicious code through the Internet requires the assistance of service providers as a conduit, a service provider that does not have the criminal intent cannot incur liability under this section. Thus, there is no duty on a service provider to actively monitor content to avoid criminal liability under this provision.

120. With respect to paragraph 2 on attempt, some offences defined in the Convention, or elements of these offences, were considered to be conceptually

difficult to attempt (for example, the elements of offering or making available of child pornography). Moreover, some legal systems limit the offences for which the attempt is punished. Accordingly, it is only required that the attempt be criminalised with respect to offences established in accordance with Articles 3, 4, 5, 7, 8, 9(1)(a) and 9(1)(c).

121. As with all the offences established in accordance with the Convention, attempt and aiding or abetting must be committed intentionally.

122. Paragraph 3 was added to address the difficulties Parties may have with paragraph 2, given the widely varying concepts in different legislations and despite the effort in paragraph 2 to exempt certain aspects from the provision on attempt. A Party may declare that it reserves the right not to apply paragraph 2 in part or in whole. This means that any Party making a reservation as to that provision will have no obligation to criminalise attempt at all, or may select the offences or parts of offences to which it will attach criminal sanctions in relation to attempt. The reservation aims at enabling the widest possible ratification of the Convention while permitting Parties to preserve some of their fundamental legal concepts.

Corporate liability (Article 12)

123. Article 12 deals with the liability of legal persons. It is consistent with the current legal trend to recognise corporate liability. It is intended to impose liability on corporations, associations and similar legal persons for the criminal actions undertaken by a

person in a leading position within such legal person, where undertaken for the benefit of that legal person. Article 12 also contemplates liability where such a leading person fails to supervise or control an employee or an agent of the legal person, where such failure facilitates the commission by that employee or agent of one of the offences established in the Convention.

124. Under paragraph 1, four conditions need to be met for liability to attach. First, one of the offences described in the Convention must have been committed. Second, the offence must have been committed for the benefit of the legal person. Third, a person who has a leading position must have committed the offence (including aiding and abetting). The term "person who has a leading position" refers to a natural person who has a high position in the organisation, such as a director. Fourth, the person who has a leading position must have acted on the basis of one of these powers - a power of representation or an authority to take decisions or to exercise control - which demonstrate that such a physical person acted within the scope of his or her authority to engage the liability of the legal person. In sum, paragraph 1 obligates Parties to have the ability to impose liability on the legal person only for offences committed by such leading persons.

125. In addition, Paragraph 2 obligates Parties to have the ability to impose liability upon a legal person where the crime is committed not by the leading person described in paragraph 1, but by another person acting under the legal person's authority, i.e., one of its employees or agents acting within the scope of their authority. The conditions that must be fulfilled

before liability can attach are that (1) an offence has been committed by such an employee or agent of the legal person, (2) the offence has been committed for the benefit of the legal person; and (3) the commission of the offence has been made possible by the leading person having failed to supervise the employee or agent. In this context, failure to supervise should be interpreted to include failure to take appropriate and reasonable measures to prevent employees or agents from committing criminal activities on behalf of the legal person. Such appropriate and reasonable measures could be determined by various factors, such as the type of the business, its size, the standards or the established business best practices, etc. This should not be interpreted as requiring a general surveillance regime over employee communications (s. service provider does not incur liability by virtue of the fact that a crime was committed on its system by a customer, user or other third person, because the term "acting under its authority" applies exclusively to employees and agents acting within the scope of their authority.

126. Liability under this Article may be criminal, civil or administrative. Each Party has the flexibility to choose to provide for any or all of these forms of liability, in accordance with the legal principles of each Party, as long as it meets the criteria of Article 13, paragraph 2, that the sanction or measure be "effective, proportionate and dissuasive" and includes monetary sanctions.

127. Paragraph 4 clarifies that corporate liability does not exclude individual liability.

Sanctions and measures (Article 13)

128. This article is closely related to Articles 2-11, which define various computer- or computer-related crimes that should be made punishable under criminal law. In accordance with the obligations imposed by those articles, this provision obliges the Contracting Parties to draw consequences from the serious nature of these offences by providing for criminal sanctions that are 'effective, proportionate and dissuasive' and, in the case of natural persons, include the possibility of imposing prison sentences.

129. Legal persons whose liability is to be established in accordance with Article 12 shall also be subject to sanctions that are 'effective, proportionate and dissuasive', which can be criminal, administrative or civil in nature. Contracting Parties are compelled, under paragraph 2, to provide for the possibility of imposing monetary sanctions on legal persons.

130. The article leaves open the possibility of other sanctions or measures reflecting the seriousness of the offences, for example, measures could include injunction or forfeiture. It leaves to the Parties the discretionary power to create a system of criminal offences and sanctions that is compatible with their existing national legal systems.

Section 2 - Procedural law

131. The articles in this Section describe certain procedural measures to be taken at the national level for the purpose of criminal investigation of the offences established in Section 1, other criminal offences

committed by means of a computer system and the collection of evidence in electronic form of a criminal offence. In accordance with Article 39, paragraph 3, nothing in the Convention requires or invites a Party to establish powers or procedures other than those contained in this Convention, nor precludes a Party from doing so.

132. The technological revolution, which encompasses the "electronic highway" where numerous forms of communication and services are interrelated and interconnected through the sharing of common transmission media and carriers, has altered the sphere of criminal law and criminal procedure. The ever-expanding network of communications opens new doors for criminal activity in respect of both traditional offences and new technological crimes. Not only must substantive criminal law keep abreast of these new abuses, but so must criminal procedural law and investigative techniques. Equally, safeguards should also be adapted or developed to keep abreast of the new technological environment and new procedural powers.

133. One of the major challenges in combating crime in the networked environment is the difficulty in identifying the perpetrator and assessing the extent and impact of the criminal act. A further problem is caused by the volatility of electronic data, which may be altered, moved or deleted in seconds. For example, a user who is in control of the data may use the computer system to erase the data that is the subject of a criminal investigation, thereby destroying the evidence. Speed and, sometimes, secrecy are often vital for the success of an investigation.

134. The Convention adapts traditional procedural measures, such as search and seizure, to the new technological environment. Additionally, new measures have been created, such as expedited preservation of data, in order to ensure that traditional measures of collection, such as search and seizure, remain effective in the volatile technological environment. As data in the new technological environment is not always static, but may be flowing in the process of communication, other traditional collection procedures relevant to telecommunications, such as real-time collection of traffic data and interception of content data, have also been adapted in order to permit the collection of electronic data that is in the process of communication. Some of these measures are set out in Council of Europe Recommendation No. R (95) 13 on problems of criminal procedural law connected with information technology.

135. All the provisions referred to in this Section aim at permitting the obtaining or collection of data for the purpose of specific criminal investigations or proceedings. The drafters of the present Convention discussed whether the Convention should impose an obligation for service providers to routinely collect and retain traffic data for a certain fixed period of time, but did not include any such obligation due to lack of consensus.

136. The procedures in general refer to all types of data, including three specific types of computer data (traffic data, content data and subscriber data), which may exist in two forms (stored or in the process of communication). Definitions of some of

these terms are provided in Articles 1 and 18. The applicability of a procedure to a particular type or form of electronic data depends on the nature and form of the data and the nature of the procedure, as specifically described in each article.

137. In adapting traditional procedural laws to the new technological environment, the question of appropriate terminology arises in the provisions of this section. The options included maintaining traditional language ('search' and 'seize'), using new and more technologically oriented computer terms ('access' and 'copy'), as adopted in texts of other international fora on the subject (such as the G8 High Tech Crime Subgroup), or employing a compromise of mixed language ('search or similarly access', and 'seize or similarly secure'). As there is a need to reflect the evolution of concepts in the electronic environment, as well as identify and maintain their traditional roots, the flexible approach of allowing States to use either the old notions of "search and seizure" or the new notions of "access and copying" is employed.

138. All the articles in the Section refer to "competent authorities" and the powers they shall be granted for the purposes of specific criminal investigations or proceedings. In certain countries, only judges have the power to order or authorise the collection or production of evidence, while in other countries prosecutors or other law enforcement officers are entrusted with the same or similar powers. Therefore, 'competent authority' refers to a judicial, administrative or other law enforcement authority that is empowered by domestic law to order, authorise or undertake the execution of procedural

measures for the purpose of collection or production of evidence with respect to specific criminal investigations or proceedings.

Title 1 – Common provisions

139. The Section begins with two provisions of a general nature that apply to all the articles relating to procedural law.

Scope of procedural provisions (Article 14)

140. Each State Party is obligated to adopt such legislative and other measures as may be necessary, in accordance with its domestic law and legal framework, to establish the powers and procedures described in this Section for the purpose of "specific criminal investigations or proceedings."

141. Subject to two exceptions, each Party shall apply the powers and procedures established in accordance with this Section to: (i) criminal offences established in accordance with Section 1 of the Convention; (ii) other criminal offences committed by means of a computer system; and (iii) the collection of evidence in electronic form of a criminal offence. Thus, for the purpose of specific criminal investigations or proceedings, the powers and procedures referred to in this Section shall be applied to offences established in accordance with the Convention, to other criminal offences committed by means of a computer system, and to the collection of evidence in electronic form of a criminal offence. This ensures that evidence in electronic form of any criminal offence can be obtained or collected by means of the powers and procedures set out in this Section. It ensures an

equivalent or parallel capability for the obtaining or collection of computer data as exists under traditional powers and procedures for non-electronic data. The Convention makes it explicit that Parties should incorporate into their laws the possibility that information contained in digital or other electronic form can be used as evidence before a court in criminal proceedings, irrespective of the nature of the criminal offence that is prosecuted.

142. There are two exceptions to this scope of application. First, Article 21 provides that the power to intercept content data shall be limited to a range of serious offences to be determined by domestic law. Many States limit the power of interception of oral communications or telecommunications to a range of serious offences, in recognition of the privacy of oral communications and telecommunications and the intrusiveness of this investigative measure. Likewise, this Convention only requires Parties to establish interception powers and procedures in relation to content data of specified computer communications in respect of a range of serious offences to be determined by domestic law.

143. Second, a Party may reserve the right to apply the measures in Article 20 (real-time collection of traffic data) only to offences or categories of offences specified in the reservation, provided that the range of such offences or categories is not more restricted than the range of offences to which it applies the interception measures referred to in Article 21. Some States consider the collection of traffic data as being equivalent to the collection of content data in terms of privacy and intrusiveness. The right of reservation would permit these States to limit the application of

the measures to collect traffic data, in real-time, to the same range of offences to which it applies the powers and procedures of real-time interception of content data. Many States, however, do not consider the interception of content data and the collection of traffic data to be equivalent in terms of privacy interests and degree of intrusiveness, as the collection of traffic data alone does not collect or disclose the content of the communication. As the real-time collection of traffic data can be very important in tracing the source or destination of computer communications (thus, assisting in identifying criminals), the Convention invites Parties that exercise the right of reservation to limit their reservation so as to enable the broadest application of the powers and procedures provided to collect, in real-time, traffic data.

144. Paragraph (b) provides a reservation for countries which, due to existing limitations in their domestic law at the time of the Convention's adoption, cannot intercept communications on computer systems operated for the benefit of a closed group of users and which do not use public communications networks nor are they connected with other computer systems. The term "closed group of users" refers, for example, to a set of users that is limited by association to the service provider, such as the employees of a company for which the company provides the ability to communicate amongst themselves using a computer network. The term "not connected with other computer systems" means that, at the time an order under Articles 20 or 21 would be issued, the system on which communications are being transmitted does not have a physical or logical

connection to another computer network. The term "does not employ public communications networks" excludes systems that use public computer networks (including the Internet), public telephone networks or other public telecommunications facilities in transmitting communications, whether or not such use is apparent to the users.

Conditions and safeguards (Article 15)

145. The establishment, implementation and application of the powers and procedures provided for in this Section of the Convention shall be subject to the conditions and safeguards provided for under the domestic law of each Party. Although Parties are obligated to introduce certain procedural law provisions into their domestic law, the modalities of establishing and implementing these powers and procedures into their legal system, and the application of the powers and procedures in specific cases, are left to the domestic law and procedures of each Party. These domestic laws and procedures, as more specifically described below, shall include conditions or safeguards, which may be provided constitutionally, legislatively, judicially or otherwise. The modalities should include the addition of certain elements as conditions or safeguards that balance the requirements of law enforcement with the protection of human rights and liberties. As the Convention applies to Parties of many different legal systems and cultures, it is not possible to specify in detail the applicable conditions and safeguards for each power or procedure. Parties shall ensure that these conditions and safeguards provide for the

adequate protection of human rights and liberties. There are some common standards or minimum safeguards to which Parties to the Convention must adhere. These include standards or minimum safeguards arising pursuant to obligations that a Party has undertaken under applicable international human rights instruments. These instruments include the 1950 European Convention for the Protection of Human Rights and Fundamental Freedoms and its additional Protocols No. 1, 4, 6, 7 and 12 (ETS N°s 005 (4), 009, 046, 114, 117 and 177), in respect of European States that are Parties to them. It also includes other applicable human rights instruments in respect of States in other regions of the world (e.g. the 1969 American Convention on Human Rights and the 1981 African Charter on Human Rights and Peoples' Rights) which are Parties to these instruments, as well as the more universally ratified 1966 International Covenant on Civil and Political Rights. In addition, there are similar protections provided under the laws of most States.

146. Another safeguard in the convention is that the powers and procedures shall "incorporate the principle of proportionality." Proportionality shall be implemented by each Party in accordance with relevant principles of its domestic law. For European countries, this will be derived from the principles of the 1950 Council of Europe Convention for the Protection of Human Rights and Fundamental Freedoms, its applicable jurisprudence and national legislation and jurisprudence, that the power or procedure shall be proportional to the nature and circumstances of the offence. Other States will apply

related principles of their law, such as limitations on overbreadth of production orders and reasonableness requirements for searches and seizures. Also, the explicit limitation in Article 21 that the obligations regarding interception measures are with respect to a range of serious offences, determined by domestic law, is an explicit example of the application of the proportionality principle.

147. Without limiting the types of conditions and safeguards that could be applicable, the Convention requires specifically that such conditions and safeguards include, as appropriate in view of the nature of the power or procedure, judicial or other independent supervision, grounds justifying the application of the power or procedure and the limitation on the scope or the duration thereof. National legislatures will have to determine, in applying binding international obligations and established domestic principles, which of the powers and procedures are sufficiently intrusive in nature to require implementation of particular conditions and safeguards. As stated in Paragraph 215, Parties should clearly apply conditions and safeguards such as these with respect to interception, given its intrusiveness. At the same time, for example, such safeguards need not apply equally to preservation. Other safeguards that should be addressed under domestic law include the right against self-incrimination, and legal privileges and specificity of individuals or places which are the object of the application of the measure.

148. With respect to the matters discussed in paragraph 3, of primary importance is consideration of the "public interest", in particular the interests of "the sound

administration of justice". To the extent consistent with the public interest, Parties should consider other factors, such as the impact of the power or procedure on "the rights, responsibilities and legitimate interests" of third parties, including service providers, incurred as a result of the enforcement measures, and whether appropriate means can be taken to mitigate such impact. In sum, initial consideration is given to the sound administration of justice and other public interests (e.g. public safety and public health and other interests, including the interests of victims and the respect for private life). To the extent consistent with the public interest, consideration would ordinarily also be given to such issues as minimising disruption of consumer services, protection from liability for disclosure or facilitating disclosure under this Chapter, or protection of proprietary interests.

Title 2 – Expedited preservation of stored computer data

149. The measures in Articles 16 and 17 apply to stored data that has already been collected and retained by data-holders, such as service providers. They do not apply to the real-time collection and retention of future traffic data or to real-time access to the content of communications. These issues are addressed in Title 5.

150. The measures described in the articles operate only where computer data already exists and is currently being stored. For many reasons, computer data relevant for criminal investigations may not exist or no longer be stored. For example, accurate data may not have been collected and retained, or if collected was not maintained. Data protection laws may have affirmatively required the destruction of important

data before anyone realised its significance for criminal proceedings. Sometimes there may be no business reason for the collection and retention of data, such as where customers pay a flat rate for services or the services are free. Article 16 and 17 do not address these problems.

151. "Data preservation" must be distinguished from "data retention". While sharing similar meanings in common language, they have distinctive meanings in relation to computer usage. To preserve data means to keep data, which already exists in a stored form, protected from anything that would cause its current quality or condition to change or deteriorate. To retain data means to keep data, which is currently being generated, in one's possession into the future. Data retention connotes the accumulation of data in the present and the keeping or possession of it into a future time period. Data retention is the process of storing data. Data preservation, on the other hand, is the activity that keeps that stored data secure and safe.

152. Articles 16 and 17 refer only to data preservation, and not data retention. They do not mandate the collection and retention of all, or even some, data collected by a service provider or other entity in the course of its activities. The preservation measures apply to computer data that "has been stored by means of a computer system", which presupposes that the data already exists, has already been collected and is stored. Furthermore, as indicated in Article 14, all of the powers and procedures required to be established in Section 2 of the Convention are 'for the purpose of specific criminal investigations or proceedings', which limits the application of the

measures to an investigation in a particular case. Additionally, where a Party gives effect to preservation measures by means of an order, this order is in relation to "specified stored computer data in the person's possession or control" (paragraph 2). The articles, therefore, provide only for the power to require preservation of existing stored data, pending subsequent disclosure of the data pursuant to other legal powers, in relation to specific criminal investigations or proceedings.

153. The obligation to ensure preservation of data is not intended to require Parties to restrict the offering or use of services that do not routinely collect and retain certain types of data, such as traffic or subscriber data, as part of their legitimate business practices. Neither does it require them to implement new technical capabilities in order to do so, e.g. to preserve ephemeral data, which may be present on the system for such a brief period that it could not be reasonably preserved in response to a request or an order.

154. Some States have laws that require that certain types of data, such as personal data, held by particular types of holders must not be retained and must be deleted if there is no longer a business purpose for the retention of the data. In the European Union, the general principle is implemented by Directive 95/46/EC and, in the particular context of the telecommunications sector, Directive 97/66/EC. These directives establish the obligation to delete data as soon as its storage is no longer necessary. However, member States may adopt legislation to provide for exemptions when necessary for the purpose of the prevention, investigation or

prosecution of criminal offences. These directives do not prevent member States of the European Union from establishing powers and procedures under their domestic law to preserve specified data for specific investigations.

155. Data preservation is for most countries an entirely new legal power or procedure in domestic law. It is an important new investigative tool in addressing computer and computer-related crime, especially crimes committed through the Internet. First, because of the volatility of computer data, the data is easily subject to manipulation or change. Thus, valuable evidence of a crime can be easily lost through careless handling and storage practices, intentional manipulation or deletion designed to destroy evidence or routine deletion of data that is no longer required to be retained. One method of preserving its integrity is for competent authorities to search or similarly access and seize or similarly secure the data. However, where the custodian of the data is trustworthy, such as a reputable business, the integrity of the data can be secured more quickly by means of an order to preserve the data. For legitimate businesses, a preservation order may also be less disruptive to its normal activities and reputation than the execution of a search and seizure of its premises. Second, computer and computer-related crimes are committed to a great extent as a result of the transmission of communications through the computer system. These communications may contain illegal content, such as child pornography, computer viruses or other instructions that cause interference with data or the proper functioning of the computer system, or evidence of the commission

of other crimes, such as drug trafficking or fraud. Determining the source or destination of these past communications can assist in identifying the identity of the perpetrators. In order to trace these communications so as to determine their source or destination, traffic data regarding these past communications is required. Third, where these communications contain illegal content or evidence of criminal activity and copies of such communications are retained by service providers, such as e-mail, the preservation of these communications is important in order to ensure that critical evidence is not lost. Obtaining copies of these past communications (e.g., stored e-mail that has been sent or received) can reveal evidence of criminality.

156. The power of expedited preservation of computer data is intended to address these problems. Parties are therefore required to introduce a power to order the preservation of specified computer data as a provisional measure, whereby data will be preserved for a period of time as long as necessary, up to a maximum of 90 days. A Party may provide for subsequent renewal of the order. This does not mean that the data is disclosed to law enforcement authorities at the time of preservation. For this to happen, an additional measure of disclosure or a search has to be ordered. With respect to disclosure to law enforcement of preserved data, see paragraphs 152 and 160.

157. It is also important that preservation measures exists at the national level in order to enable Parties to assist one another at the international level with expedited preservation of stored data located in their

territory. This will help to ensure that critical data is not lost during often time-consuming traditional mutual legal assistance procedures that enable the requested Party to actually obtain the data and disclose it to the requesting Party.

Expedited preservation of stored computer data (Article 16)

158. Article 16 aims at ensuring that national competent authorities are able to order or similarly obtain the expedited preservation of specified stored computer-data in connection with a specific criminal investigation or proceeding.

159. 'Preservation' requires that data, which already exists in a stored form, be protected from anything that would cause its current quality or condition to change or deteriorate. It requires that it be kept safe from modification, deterioration or deletion. Preservation does not necessarily mean that the data be 'frozen' (i.e. rendered inaccessible) and that it, or copies thereof, cannot be used by legitimate users. The person to whom the order is addressed may, depending on the exact specifications of the order, still access the data. The article does not specify how data should be preserved. It is left to each Party to determine the appropriate manner of preservation and whether, in some appropriate cases, preservation of the data should also entail its 'freezing'.

160. The reference to 'order or similarly obtain' is intended to allow the use of other legal methods of achieving preservation than merely by means of a judicial or administrative order or directive (e.g. from

police or prosecutor). In some States, preservation orders do not exist in their procedural law, and data can only be preserved and obtained through search and seizure or production order. Flexibility is intended by the use of the phrase 'or otherwise obtain' to permit these States to implement this article by the use of these means. However, it is recommended that States consider the establishment of powers and procedures to actually order the recipient of the order to preserve the data, as quick action by this person can result in the more expeditious implementation of the preservation measures in particular cases.

161. The power to order or similarly obtain the expeditious preservation of specified computer data applies to any type of stored computer data. This can include any type of data that is specified in the order to be preserved. It can include, for example, business, health, personal or other records. The measures are to be established by Parties for use "in particular where there are grounds to believe that the computer data is particularly vulnerable to loss or modification." This can include situations where the data is subject to a short period of retention, such as where there is a business policy to delete the data after a certain period of time or the data is ordinarily deleted when the storage medium is used to record other data. It can also refer to the nature of the custodian of the data or the insecure manner in which the data is stored. However, if the custodian were untrustworthy, it would be more secure to effect preservation by means of search and seizure, rather than by means of an order that could be disobeyed. A specific reference to "traffic data" is made in

paragraph 1 in order to signal the provisions particular applicability to this type of data, which if collected and retained by a service provider, is usually held for only a short period of time. The reference to "traffic data" also provides a link between the measures in Article 16 and 17.

162. Paragraph 2 specifies that where a Party gives effect to preservation by means of an order, the order to preserve is in relation to "specified stored computer data in the person's possession or control". Thus, the stored data may actually be in the possession of the person or it may be stored elsewhere but subject to the control of this person. The person who receives the order is obliged "to preserve and maintain the integrity of that computer data for a period of time as long as necessary, up to a maximum of 90 days, to enable the competent authorities to seek its disclosure." The domestic law of a Party should specify a maximum period of time for which data, subject to an order, must be preserved, and the order should specify the exact period of time that the specified data is to be preserved. The period of time should be as long as necessary, up to a maximum of 90 days, to permit the competent authorities to undertake other legal measures, such as search and seizure, or similar access or securing, or the issuance of a production order, to obtain the disclosure of the data. A Party may provide for subsequent renewal of the production order. In this context, reference should be made to Article 29, which concerns a mutual assistance request to obtain the expeditious preservation of data stored by means of a computer system. That article specifies that preservation effected in response to a mutual assistance request

"shall be for a period not less than 60 days in order to enable the requesting Party to submit a request for the search or similar access, seizure or similar securing, or disclosure of the data."

163. Paragraph 3 imposes an obligation of confidentiality regarding the undertaking of preservation procedures on the custodian of the data to be preserved, or on the person ordered to preserve the data, for a period of time as established in domestic law. This requires Parties to introduce confidentiality measures in respect of expedited preservation of stored data, and a time limit in respect of the period of confidentiality. This measure accommodates the needs of law enforcement so that the suspect of the investigation is not made aware of the investigation, as well as the right of individuals to privacy. For law enforcement authorities, the expedited preservation of data forms part of initial investigations and, therefore, covertness may be important at this stage. Preservation is a preliminary measure pending the taking of other legal measures to obtain the data or its disclosure. Confidentiality is required in order that other persons do not attempt to tamper with or delete the data. For the person to whom the order is addressed, the data subject or other persons who may be mentioned or identified in the data, there is a clear time limit to the length of the measure. The dual obligations to keep the data safe and secure and to maintain confidentiality of the fact that the preservation measure has been undertaken helps to protect the privacy of the data subject or other persons who may be mentioned or identified in that data.

164. In addition to the limitations set out above, the powers and procedures referred to in Article 16 are

also subject to the conditions and safeguards provided in Articles 14 and 15.

Expedited preservation and partial disclosure of traffic data (Article 17)

165. This article establishes specific obligations in relation to the preservation of traffic data under Article 16 and provides for expeditious disclosure of some traffic data so as to identify that other service providers were involved in the transmission of specified communications. "Traffic data" is defined in Article 1.

166. Obtaining stored traffic data that is associated with past communications may be critical in determining the source or destination of a past communication, which is crucial to identifying the persons who, for example, have distributed child pornography, distributed fraudulent misrepresentations as part of a fraudulent scheme, distributed computer viruses, attempted or successfully accessed illegally computer systems, or transmitted communications to a computer system that have interfered either with data in the system or with the proper functioning of the system. However, this data is frequently stored for only short periods of time, as laws designed to protect privacy may prohibit or market forces may discourage the long-term storage of such data. Therefore, it is important that preservation measures be undertaken to secure the integrity of this data.

167. Often more than one service provider may be involved in the transmission of a communication. Each service provider may possess some traffic data

related to the transmission of the specified communication, which either has been generated and retained by that service provider in relation to the passage of the communication through its system or has been provided from other service providers. Sometimes traffic data, or at least some types of traffic data, are shared among the service providers involved in the transmission of the communication for commercial, security, or technical purposes. In such a case, any one of the service providers may possess the crucial traffic data that is needed to determine the source or destination of the communication. Often, however, no single service provider possesses enough of the crucial traffic data to be able to determine the actual source or destination of the communication. Each possesses one part of the puzzle, and each of these parts needs to be examined in order to identify the source or destination.

168. Article 17 ensures that where one or more service providers were involved in the transmission of a communication, expeditious preservation of traffic data can be effected among all of the service providers. The article does not specify the means by which this may be achieved, leaving it to domestic law to determine a means that is consistent with its legal and economic system. One means to achieve expeditious preservation would be for competent authorities to serve expeditiously a separate preservation order on each service provider. Nevertheless, obtaining a series of separate orders can be unduly time consuming. A preferred alternative could be to obtain a single order, the scope of which however would apply to all service

providers that were identified subsequently as being involved in the transmission of the specific communication. This comprehensive order could be served sequentially on each service provider identified. Other possible alternatives could involve the participation of service providers. For example, requiring a service provider that was served with an order to notify the next service provider in the chain of the existence and terms of the preservation order. This notice could, depending on domestic law, have the effect of either permitting the other service provider to preserve voluntarily the relevant traffic data, despite any obligations to delete it, or mandating the preservation of the relevant traffic data. The second service provider could similarly notify the next service provider in the chain.

169. As traffic data is not disclosed to law enforcement authorities upon service of a preservation order to a service provider (but only obtained or disclosed subsequently upon the taking of other legal measures), these authorities will not know whether the service provider possesses all of the crucial traffic data or whether there were other service providers involved in the chain of transmitting the communication. Therefore, this article requires that the service provider, which receives a preservation order or similar measure, disclose expeditiously to the competent authorities, or other designated person, a sufficient amount of traffic data to enable the competent authorities to identify any other service providers and the path through which the communication was transmitted. The competent authorities should specify clearly the type of traffic data that is required to be disclosed. Receipt of this

information would enable the competent authorities to determine whether to take preservation measures with respect to the other service providers. In this way, the investigating authorities can trace the communication back to its origin, or forward to its destination, and identify the perpetrator or perpetrators of the specific crime being investigated. The measures in this article are also subject to the limitations, conditions and safeguards provided in Articles 14 and 15.

Title 3 – Production order

Production order (Article 18)

170. Paragraph 1 of this article calls for Parties to enable their competent authorities to compel a person in its territory to provide specified stored computer data, or a service provider offering its services in the territory of the Party to submit subscriber information. The data in question are stored or existing data, and do not include data that has not yet come into existence such as traffic data or content data related to future communications. Instead of requiring States to apply systematically coercive measures in relation to third parties, such as search and seizure of data, it is essential that States have within their domestic law alternative investigative powers that provide a less intrusive means of obtaining information relevant to criminal investigations.

171. A "production order" provides a flexible measure which law enforcement can apply in many cases, especially instead of measures that are more intrusive

or more onerous. The implementation of such a procedural mechanism will also be beneficial to third party custodians of data, such as ISPs, who are often prepared to assist law enforcement authorities on a voluntary basis by providing data under their control, but who prefer an appropriate legal basis for such assistance, relieving them of any contractual or non-contractual liability.

172. The production order refers to computer data or subscriber information that are in the possession or control of a person or a service provider. The measure is applicable only to the extent that the person or service provider maintains such data or information. Some service providers, for example, do not keep records regarding the subscribers to their services.

173. Under paragraph 1(a), a Party shall ensure that its competent law enforcement authorities have the power to order a person in its territory to submit specified computer data stored in a computer system, or data storage medium that is in that person's possession or control. The term "possession or control" refers to physical possession of the data concerned in the ordering Party's territory, and situations in which the data to be produced is outside of the person's physical possession but the person can nonetheless freely control production of the data from within the ordering Party's territory (for example, subject to applicable privileges, a person who is served with a production order for information stored in his or her account by means of a remote online storage service, must produce such information). At the same time, a mere technical ability to access remotely stored data (e.g. the ability

of a user to access through a network link remotely stored data not within his or her legitimate control) does not necessarily constitute "control" within the meaning of this provision. In some States, the concept denominated under law as "possession" covers physical and constructive possession with sufficient breadth to meet this "possession or control" requirement.

Under paragraph 1(b), a Party shall also provide for the power to order a service provider offering services in its territory to "submit subscriber information in the service provider's possession or control". As in paragraph 1(a), the term "possession or control" refers to subscriber information in the service provider's physical possession and to remotely stored subscriber information under the service provider's control (for example at a remote data storage facility provided by another company). The term "relating to such service" means that the power is to be available for the purpose of obtaining subscriber information relating to services offered in the ordering Party's territory.

174. The conditions and safeguards referred to in paragraph 2 of the article, depending on the domestic law of each Party, may exclude privileged data or information. A Party may wish to prescribe different terms, different competent authorities and different safeguards concerning the submission of particular types of computer data or subscriber information held by particular categories of persons or service providers. For example, with respect to some types of data, such as publicly available subscriber information, a Party might permit law enforcement agents to issue such an order where in other situations a court order could be required. On the

other hand, in some situations a Party might require, or be mandated by human rights safeguards to require that a production order be issued only by judicial authorities in order to be able to obtain certain types of data. Parties may wish to limit the disclosure of this data for law enforcement purposes to situations where a production order to disclose such information has been issued by judicial authorities. The proportionality principle also provides some flexibility in relation to the application of the measure, for instance in many States in order to exclude its application in minor cases.

175. A further consideration for Parties is the possible inclusion of measures concerning confidentiality. The provision does not contain a specific reference to confidentiality, in order to maintain the parallel with the non-electronic world where confidentiality is not imposed in general regarding production orders. However, in the electronic, particularly on-line, world a production order can sometimes be employed as a preliminary measure in the investigation, preceding further measures such as search and seizure or real-time interception of other data. Confidentiality could be essential for the success of the investigation.

176. With respect to the modalities of production, Parties could establish obligations that the specified computer data or subscriber information must be produced in the manner specified in the order. This could include reference to a time period within which disclosure must be made, or to form, such as that the data or information be provided in "plain text", on-line or on a paper print-out or on a diskette.

177. "Subscriber information" is defined in paragraph 3. In principle, it refers to any information held by the administration of a service provider relating to a subscriber to its services. Subscriber information may be contained in the form of computer data or any other form, such as paper records. As subscriber information includes forms of data other than just computer data, a special provision has been included in the article to address this type of information. "Subscriber" is intended to include a broad range of service provider clients, from persons holding paid subscriptions, to those paying on a per-use basis, to those receiving free services. It also includes information concerning persons entitled to use the subscriber's account.

178. In the course of a criminal investigation, subscriber information may be needed primarily in two specific situations. First, subscriber information is needed to identify which services and related technical measures have been used or are being used by a subscriber, such as the type of telephone service used (e.g., mobile), type of other associated services used (e.g., call forwarding, voice-mail, etc.), telephone number or other technical address (e.g., e-mail address). Second, when a technical address is known, subscriber information is needed in order to assist in establishing the identity of the person concerned. Other subscriber information, such as commercial information about billing and payment records of the subscriber may also be relevant to criminal investigations, especially where the crime under investigation involves computer fraud or other economic crimes.

179. Therefore, subscriber information includes various types of information about the use of a service and the user of that service. With respect to the use of the service, the term means any information, other than traffic or content data, by which can be established the type of communication service used, the technical provisions related thereto, and the period of time during which the person subscribed to the service. The term 'technical provisions' includes all measures taken to enable a subscriber to enjoy the communication service offered. Such provisions include the reservation of a technical number or address (telephone number, web site address or domain name, e-mail address, etc.), as well as the provision and registration of communication equipment used by the subscriber, such as telephone devices, call centers or LANs (local area networks).

180. Subscriber information is not limited to information directly related to the use of the communication service. It also means any information, other than traffic data or content data, by which can be established the user's identity, postal or geographic address, telephone and other access number, and billing and payment information, which is available on the basis of the service agreement or arrangement between the subscriber and the service provider. It also means any other information, other than traffic data or content data, concerning the site or location where the communication equipment is installed, which is available on the basis of the service agreement or arrangement. This latter information may only be relevant in practical terms where the equipment is not portable, but knowledge as to the portability or purported location of the equipment

(on the basis of the information provided according to the service agreement or arrangement) can be instrumental to an investigation.

181. However, this article should not be understood as to impose an obligation on service providers to keep records of their subscribers, nor would it require service providers to ensure the correctness of such information. Thus, a service provider is not obliged to register identity information of users of so-called prepaid cards for mobile telephone services. Nor is it obliged to verify the identity of the subscribers or to resist the use of pseudonyms by users of its services.

182. As the powers and procedures in this Section are for the purpose of specific criminal investigations or proceedings (Article 14), production orders are to be used in individual cases concerning, usually, particular subscribers. For example, on the basis of the provision of a particular name mentioned in the production order, a particular associated telephone number or e-mail address may be requested. On the basis of a particular telephone number or e-mail address, the name and address of the subscriber concerned may be ordered. The provision does not authorise Parties to issue a legal order to disclose indiscriminate amounts of the service provider's subscriber information about groups of subscribers e.g. for the purpose of data-mining.

183. The reference to a "service agreement or arrangement" should be interpreted in a broad sense and includes any kind of relationship on the basis of which a client uses the provider's services.

Title 4 – Search and seizure of stored computer data

Search and seizure of stored computer data (Article 19)

184. This article aims at modernising and harmonising domestic laws on search and seizure of stored computer data for the purposes of obtaining evidence with respect to specific criminal investigations or proceedings. Any domestic criminal procedural law includes powers for search and seizure of tangible objects. However, in a number of jurisdictions stored computer data per se will not be considered as a tangible object and therefore cannot be secured on behalf of criminal investigations and proceedings in a parallel manner as tangible objects, other than by securing the data medium upon which it is stored. The aim of Article 19 of this Convention is to establish an equivalent power relating to stored data.

185. In the traditional search environment concerning documents or records, a search involves gathering evidence that has been recorded or registered in the past in tangible form, such as ink on paper. The investigators search or inspect such recorded data, and seize or physically take away the tangible record. The gathering of data takes place during the period of the search and in respect of data that exists at that time. The precondition for obtaining legal authority to undertake a search is the existence of grounds to believe, as prescribed by domestic law and human rights safeguards, that such data exists in a particular location and will afford evidence of a specific criminal offence.

186. With respect to the search for evidence, in particular computer data, in the new technological environment, many of the characteristics of a

traditional search remain. For example, the gathering of the data occurs during the period of the search and in respect of data that exists at that time. The preconditions for obtaining legal authority to undertake a search remain the same. The degree of belief required for obtaining legal authorisation to search is not any different whether the data is in tangible form or in electronic form. Likewise, the belief and the search are in respect of data that already exists and that will afford evidence of a specific offence.

187. However, with respect to the search of computer data, additional procedural provisions are necessary in order to ensure that computer data can be obtained in a manner that is equally effective as a search and seizure of a tangible data carrier. There are several reasons for this: first, the data is in intangible form, such as in an electromagnetic form. Second, while the data may be read with the use of computer equipment, it cannot be seized and taken away in the same sense as can a paper record. The physical medium on which the intangible data is stored (e.g., the computer hard-drive or a diskette) must be seized and taken away, or a copy of the data must be made in either tangible form (e.g., computer print-out) or intangible form, on a physical medium (e.g., diskette), before the tangible medium containing the copy can be seized and taken away. In the latter two situations, where such copies of the data are made, a copy of the data remains in the computer system or storage device. Domestic law should provide for a power to make such copies. Third, due to the connectivity of computer systems, data may not be stored in the particular computer

that is searched, but such data may be readily accessible to that system. It could be stored in an associated data storage device that is connected directly to the computer, or connected to the computer indirectly through communication systems, such as the Internet. This may or may not require new laws to permit an extension of the search to where the data is actually stored (or the retrieval of the data from that site to the computer being searched), or the use traditional search powers in a more co-ordinated and expeditious manner at both locations.

188. Paragraph 1 requires Parties to empower law enforcement authorities to access and search computer data, which is contained either within a computer system or part of it (such as a connected data storage device), or on an independent data storage medium (such as a CD-ROM or diskette). As the definition of "computer system" in article 1 refers to "any device or a group of inter-connected or related devices", paragraph 1 concerns the search of a computer system and its related components that can be considered together as forming one distinct computer system (e.g., a PC together with a printer and related storage devices, or a local area network). Sometimes data that is physically stored in another system or storage device can be legally accessed through the searched computer system by establishing a connection with other distinct computer systems. This situation, involving linkages with other computer systems by means of telecommunication networks within the same territory (e.g., wide area network or Internet), is addressed at paragraph 2.

189. Although search and seizure of a "computer-data storage medium in which computer data may be stored" (paragraph 1 (b)) may be undertaken by use of traditional search powers, often the execution of a computer search requires both the search of the computer system and any related computer-data storage medium (e.g., diskettes) in the immediate vicinity of the computer system. Due to this relationship, a comprehensive legal authority is provided in paragraph 1 to encompass both situations.

190. Article 19 applies to stored computer data. In this respect, the question arises whether an unopened e-mail message waiting in the mailbox of an ISP until the addressee will download it to his or her computer system, has to be considered as stored computer data or as data in transfer. Under the law of some Parties, that e-mail message is part of a communication and therefore its content can only be obtained by applying the power of interception, whereas other legal systems consider such message as stored data to which article 19 applies. Therefore, Parties should review their laws with respect to this issue to determine what is appropriate within their domestic legal systems.

191. Reference is made to the term 'search or similarly access'. The use of the traditional word 'search' conveys the idea of the exercise of coercive power by the State, and indicates that the power referred to in this article is analogous to traditional search. 'Search' means to seek, read, inspect or review data. It includes the notions of searching for data and searching of (examining) data. On the other hand, the

word 'access' has a neutral meaning, but it reflects more accurately computer terminology. Both terms are used in order to marry the traditional concepts with modern terminology.

192. The reference to 'in its territory' is a reminder that this provision, as all the articles in this Section, concern only measures that are required to be taken at the national level.

193. Paragraph 2 allows the investigating authorities to extend their search or similar access to another computer system or part of it if they have grounds to believe that the data required is stored in that other computer system. The other computer system or part of it must, however, also be 'in its territory'.

194. The Convention does not prescribe how an extension of a search is to be permitted or undertaken. This is left to domestic law. Some examples of possible conditions are: empowering the judicial or other authority which authorised the computer search of a specific computer system, to authorise the extension of the search or similar access to a connected system if he or she has grounds to believe (to the degree required by national law and human rights safeguards) that the connected computer system may contain the specific data that is being sought; empowering the investigative authorities to extend an authorised search or similar access of a specific computer system to a connected computer system where there are similar grounds to believe that the specific data being sought is stored in the other computer system; or exercising search or similar access powers at both locations in a co-ordinated and expeditious manner. In all cases the data to be

searched must be lawfully accessible from or available to the initial computer system.

195. This article does not address 'transborder search and seizure', whereby States could search and seize data in the territory of other States without having to go through the usual channels of mutual legal assistance. This issue is discussed below at the Chapter on international co-operation.

196. Paragraph 3 addresses the issues of empowering competent authorities to seize or similarly secure computer data that has been searched or similarly accessed under paragraphs 1 or 2. This includes the power of seizure of computer hardware and computer-data storage media. In certain cases, for instance when data is stored in unique operating systems such that it cannot be copied, it is unavoidable that the data carrier as a whole has to be seized. This may also be necessary when the data carrier has to be examined in order to retrieve from it older data which was overwritten but which has, nevertheless, left traces on the data carrier.

197. In this Convention, 'seize' means to take away the physical medium upon which data or information is recorded, or to make and retain a copy of such data or information. 'Seize' includes the use or seizure of programmes needed to access the data being seized. As well as using the traditional term 'seize', the term 'similarly secure' is included to reflect other means by which intangible data is removed, rendered inaccessible or its control is otherwise taken over in the computer environment. Since the measures relate to stored intangible data, additional measures are required by competent authorities to secure the data;

that is, 'maintain the integrity of the data', or maintain the 'chain of custody' of the data, meaning that the data which is copied or removed be retained in the State in which they were found at the time of the seizure and remain unchanged during the time of criminal proceedings. The term refers to taking control over or the taking away of data.

198. The rendering inaccessible of data can include encrypting the data or otherwise technologically denying anyone access to that data. This measure could usefully be applied in situations where danger or social harm is involved, such as virus programs or instructions on how to make viruses or bombs, or where the data or their content are illegal, such as child pornography. The term 'removal' is intended to express the idea that while the data is removed or rendered inaccessible, it is not destroyed, but continues to exist. The suspect is temporarily deprived of the data, but it can be returned following the outcome of the criminal investigation or proceedings.

199. Thus, seize or similarly secure data has two functions: 1) to gather evidence, such as by copying the data, or 2) to confiscate data, such as by copying the data and subsequently rendering the original version of the data inaccessible or by removing it. The seizure does not imply a final deletion of the seized data.

200. Paragraph 4 introduces a coercive measure to facilitate the search and seizure of computer data. It addresses the practical problem that it may be difficult to access and identify the data sought as evidence, given the quantity of data that can be

processed and stored, the deployment of security measures, as well as the nature of computer operations. It recognises that system administrators, who have particular knowledge of the computer system, may need to be consulted concerning the technical modalities about how best the search should be conducted. This provision, therefore, allows law enforcement to compel a system administrator to assist, as is reasonable, the undertaking of the search and seizure.

201. This power is not only of benefit to the investigating authorities. Without such co-operation, investigative authorities could remain on the searched premises and prevent access to the computer system for long periods of time while undertaking the search. This could be an economic burden on legitimate businesses or customers and subscribers that are denied access to data during this time. A means to order the co-operation of knowledgeable persons would help in making searches more effective and cost efficient, both for law enforcement and innocent individuals affected. Legally compelling a system administrator to assist may also relieve the administrator of any contractual or other obligations not to disclose the data.

202. The information that can be ordered to be provided is that which is necessary to enable the undertaking of the search and seizure, or the similarly accessing or securing. The provision of this information, however, is restricted to that which is "reasonable". In some circumstances, reasonable provision may include disclosing a password or other security measure to the investigating authorities. However, in other circumstances, this may not be reasonable; for

example, where the disclosure of the password or other security measure would unreasonably threaten the privacy of other users or other data that is not authorised to be searched. In such case, the provision of the "necessary information" could be the disclosure, in a form that is intelligible and readable, of the actual data that is being sought by the competent authorities.

203. Under paragraph 5 of this article, the measures are subject to conditions and safeguards provided for under domestic law on the basis of Article 15 of this Convention. Such conditions may include provisions relating to the engagement and financial compensation of witnesses and experts.

204. The drafters discussed further in the frame of paragraph 5 if interested parties should be notified of the undertaking of a search procedure In the on-line world it may be less apparent that data has been searched and seized (copied) than that a seizure in the off-line world took place, where seized objects will be physically missing. The laws of some Parties do not provide for an obligation to notify in the case of a traditional search. For the Convention to require notification in respect of a computer search would create a discrepancy in the laws of these Parties. On the other hand, some Parties may consider notification as an essential feature of the measure, in order to maintain the distinction between computer search of stored data (which is generally not intended to be a surreptitious measure) and interception of flowing data (which is a surreptitious measure, see Articles 20 and 21). The issue of notification, therefore, is left to be determined by domestic law. If Parties consider a system of mandatory notification

of persons concerned, it should be borne in mind that such notification may prejudice the investigation. If such a risk exists, postponement of the notification should be considered.

Title 5 – Real-time collection of computer data

205. Articles 20 and 21 provide for the real-time collection of traffic data and the real-time interception of content data associated with specified communications transmitted by a computer system. The provisions address the real-time collection and real-time interception of such data by competent authorities, as well as their collection or interception by service providers. Obligations of confidentiality are also addressed.

206. Interception of telecommunications usually refers to traditional telecommunications networks. These networks can include cable infrastructures, whether wire or optical cable, as well as inter-connections with wireless networks, including mobile telephone systems and microwave transmission systems. Today, mobile communications are facilitated also by a system of special satellite networks. Computer networks may also consist of an independent fixed cable infrastructure, but are more frequently operated as a virtual network by connections made through telecommunication infrastructures, thus permitting the creation of computer networks or linkages of networks that are global in nature. The distinction between telecommunications and computer communications, and the distinctiveness between their infrastructures, is blurring with the convergence of telecommunication and information technologies. Thus, the definition of 'computer system' in article 1

does not restrict the manner by which the devices or group of devices may be inter-connected. Articles 20 and 21, therefore, apply to specified communications transmitted by means of a computer system, which could include transmission of the communication through telecommunication networks before it is received by another computer system.

207. Articles 20 and 21 do not make a distinction between a publicly or a privately owned telecommunication or computer system or to the use of systems and communication services offered to the public or to closed user groups or private parties. The definition of 'service provider' in Article 1 refers to public and private entities that provide to users of their services the ability to communicate by means of a computer system.

208. This Title governs the collection of evidence contained in currently generated communications, which are collected at the time of the communication (i.e., 'real time'). The data are intangible in form (e.g., in the form of transmissions of voice or electronic impulses). The flow of the data is not significantly interfered with by the collection, and the communication reaches its intended recipient. Instead of a physical seizure of the data, a recording (i.e., a copy) is made of the data being communicated. The collection of this evidence takes place during a certain period of time. A legal authority to permit the collection is sought in respect of a future event (i.e., a future transmission of data).

209. The type of data that can be collected is of two types: traffic data and content data. 'Traffic data' is defined in Article 1 d to mean any computer data relating to

a communication made by means of a computer system, which is generated by the computer system and which formed a part in the chain of communication, indicating the communication's origin, destination, route, time, date, size and duration or the type of service. 'Content data' is not defined in the Convention but refers to the communication content of the communication; i.e., the meaning or purport of the communication, or the message or information being conveyed by the communication (other than traffic data).

210. In many States, a distinction is made between the real-time interception of content data and real-time collection of traffic data in terms of both the legal prerequisites required to authorise such investigative measure and the offences in respect of which this measure can be employed. While recognising that both types of data may have associated privacy interests, many States consider that the privacy interests in respect of content data are greater due to the nature of the communication content or message. Greater limitations may be imposed with respect to the real-time collection of content data than traffic data. To assist in recognising this distinction for these States, the Convention, while operationally acknowledging that the data is collected or recorded in both situations, refers normatively in the titles of the articles to the collection of traffic data as 'real-time collection' and the collection of content data as 'real-time interception'.

211. In some States existing legislation makes no distinction between the collection of traffic data and the interception of content data, either because no

distinction has been made in the law regarding differences in privacy interests or the technological collection techniques for both measures are very similar. Thus, the legal prerequisites required to authorise the undertaking of the measures, and the offences in respect of which the measures can be employed, are the same. This situation is also recognised in the Convention by the common operational use of the term 'collect or record' in the actual text of both Articles 20 and 21.

212. With respect to the real-time interception of content data, the law often prescribes that the measure is only available in relation to the investigation of serious offences or categories of serious offences. These offences are identified in domestic law as serious for this purpose often by being named in a list of applicable offences or by being included in this category by reference to a certain maximum sentence of incarceration that is applicable to the offence. Therefore, with respect to the interception of content data, Article 21 specifically provides that Parties are only required to establish the measure 'in relation to a range of serious offences to be determined by domestic law'.

213. Article 20, concerning the collection of traffic data, on the other hand, is not so limited and in principle applies to any criminal offence covered by the Convention. However, Article 14, paragraph 3, provides that a Party may reserve the right to apply the measure only to offences or categories of offences specified in the reservation, provided that the range of offences or categories of offences is not more restricted than the range of offences to which it applies the measure of interception of content data.

Nevertheless, where such a reservation is taken, the Party shall consider restricting such reservation so as to enable the broadest range of application of the measure of collection of traffic data.

214. For some States, the offences established in the Convention would normally not be considered serious enough to permit interception of content data or, in some cases, even the collection of traffic data. Nevertheless, such techniques are often crucial for the investigation of some of the offences established in the Convention, such as those involving illegal access to computer systems, and distribution of viruses and child pornography. The source of the intrusion or distribution, for example, cannot be determined in some cases without real-time collection of traffic data. In some cases, the nature of the communication cannot be discovered without real-time interception of content data. These offences, by their nature or the means of transmission, involve the use of computer technologies. The use of technological means should, therefore, be permitted to investigate these offences. However, due to the sensitivities surrounding the issue of interception of content data, the Convention leaves the scope of this measure to be determined by domestic law. As some countries legally assimilate the collection of traffic data with the interception of content data, a reservation possibility is permitted to restrict the applicability of the former measure, but not to an extent greater than a Party restricts the measure of real-time interception of content data. Nevertheless, Parties should consider applying the two measures to the offences established by the Convention in Section 1 of Chapter II, in order to provide an effective

means for the investigation of these computer offences and computer-related offences.

215. The conditions and safeguards regarding the powers and procedures related to real-time interception of content data and real-time collection of traffic data are subject to Articles 14 and 15. As interception of content data is a very intrusive measure on private life, stringent safeguards are required to ensure an appropriate balance between the interests of justice and the fundamental rights of the individual. In the area of interception, the present Convention itself does not set out specific safeguards other than limiting authorisation of interception of content data to investigations into serious criminal offences as defined in domestic law. Nevertheless, the following important conditions and safeguards in this area, applied in domestic laws, are: judicial or other independent supervision; specificity as to the communications or persons to be intercepted; necessity, subsidiarity and proportionality (e.g. legal predicates justifying the taking of the measure; other less intrusive measures not effective); limitation on the duration of interception; right of redress. Many of these safeguards reflect the European Convention on Human Rights and its subsequent case-law (see judgements in Klass (5), Kruslin (6), Huvig (7), Malone (8), Halford (9), Lambert (10) cases). Some of these safeguards are applicable also to the collection of traffic data in real-time.

Real-time collection of traffic data (Article 20)

216. Often, historical traffic data may no longer be

available or it may not be relevant as the intruder has changed the route of communication. Therefore, the real-time collection of traffic data is an important investigative measure. Article 20 addresses the subject of real-time collection and recording of traffic data for the purpose of specific criminal investigations or proceedings.

217. Traditionally, the collection of traffic data in respect of telecommunications (e.g., telephone conversations) has been a useful investigative tool to determine the source or destination (e.g., telephone numbers) and related data (e.g., time, date and duration) of various types of illegal communications (e.g., criminal threats and harassment, criminal conspiracy, fraudulent misrepresentations) and of communications affording evidence of past or future crimes (e.g., drug trafficking, murder, economic crimes, etc.).

218. Computer communications can constitute or afford evidence of the same types of criminality. However, given that computer technology is capable of transmitting vast quantities of data, including written text, visual images and sound, it also has greater potential for committing crimes involving distribution of illegal content (e.g., child pornography). Likewise, as computers can store vast quantities of data, often of a private nature, the potential for harm, whether economic, social or personal, can be significant if the integrity of this data is interfered with. Furthermore, as the science of computer technology is founded upon the processing of data, both as an end product and as part of its operational function (e.g., execution of computer programs), any interference with this data can have

disastrous effects on the proper operation of computer systems. When an illegal distribution of child pornography, illegal access to a computer system or interference with the proper functioning of the computer system or the integrity of data, is committed, particularly from a distance such as through the Internet, it is necessary and crucial to trace the route of the communications back from the victim to the perpetrator. Therefore, the ability to collect traffic data in respect of computer communications is just as, if not more, important as it is in respect of purely traditional telecommunications. This investigative technique can correlate the time, date and source and destination of the suspect's communications with the time of the intrusions into the systems of victims, identify other victims or show links with associates.

219. Under this article, the traffic data concerned must be associated with specified communications in the territory of the Party. The specified 'communications' are in the plural, as traffic data in respect of several communications may need to be collected in order to determine the human source or destination (for example, in a household where several different persons have the use of the same telecommunications facilities, it may be necessary to correlate several communications with the individuals' opportunity to use the computer system). The communications in respect of which the traffic data may be collected or recorded, however, must be specified. Thus, the Convention does not require or authorise the general or indiscriminate surveillance and collection of large amounts of traffic data. It does not authorise the situation of 'fishing expeditions' where criminal

activities are hopefully sought to be discovered, as opposed to specific instances of criminality being investigated. The judicial or other order authorising the collection must specify the communications to which the collection of traffic data relates.

220. Subject to paragraph 2, Parties are obliged, under paragraph 1(a) to ensure that their competent authorities have the capacity to collect or record traffic data by technical means. The article does not specify technologically how the collection is to be undertaken, and no obligations in technical terms are defined.

221. In addition, under paragraph 1(b), Parties are obliged to ensure that their competent authorities have the power to compel a service provider to collect or record traffic data or to co-operate and assist the competent authorities in the collection or recording of such data. This obligation regarding service providers is applicable only to the extent that the collection or recording, or co-operation and assistance, is within the existing technical capability of the service provider. The article does not obligate service providers to ensure that they have the technical capability to undertake collections, recordings, co-operation or assistance. It does not require them to acquire or develop new equipment, hire expert support or engage in costly re-configuration of their systems. However, if their systems and personnel have the existing technical capability to provide such collection, recording, co-operation or assistance, the article would require them to take the necessary measures to engage such capability. For example, the system may be configured in such a manner, or computer programs may already be possessed by the

service provider, which would permit such measures to be taken, but they are not ordinarily executed or used in the normal course of the service provider's operation. The article would require the service provider to engage or turn-on these features, as required by law.

222. As this is a measure to be carried out at national level, the measures are applied to the collection or recording of specified communications in the territory of the Party. Thus, in practical terms, the obligations are generally applicable where the service provider has some physical infrastructure or equipment on that territory capable of undertaking the measures, although this need not be the location of its main operations or headquarters. For the purposes of this Convention, it is understood that a communication is in a Party's territory if one of the communicating parties (human beings or computers) is located in the territory or if the computer or telecommunication equipment through which the communication passes is located on the territory.

223. In general, the two possibilities for collecting traffic data in paragraph 1(a) and (b) are not alternatives. Except as provided in paragraph 2, a Party must ensure that both measures can be carried out. This is necessary because if a service provider does not have the technical ability to assume the collection or recording of traffic data (1(b)), then a Party must have the possibility for its law enforcement authorities to undertake themselves the task (1(a)). Likewise, an obligation under paragraph 1(b)(ii) to co-operate and assist the competent authorities in the collection or recording of traffic data is senseless if the competent authorities are not empowered to

collect or record themselves the traffic data. Additionally, in the situation of some local area networks (LANs), where no service provider may be involved, the only way for collection or recording to be carried out would be for the investigating authorities to do it themselves. Both measures in paragraphs 1 (a) and (b) do not have to be used each time, but the availability of both methods is required by the article.

224. This dual obligation, however, posed difficulties for certain States in which the law enforcement authorities were only able to intercept data in telecommunication systems through the assistance of a service provider, or not surreptitiously without at least the knowledge of the service provider. For this reason, paragraph 2 accommodates such a situation. Where a Party, due to the 'established principles of its domestic legal system', cannot adopt the measures referred to in paragraph 1 (a), it may instead adopt a different approach, such as only compelling service providers to provide the necessary technical facilities, to ensure the real-time collection of traffic data by law enforcement authorities. In such case, all of the other limitations regarding territory, specificity of communications and use of technical means still apply.

225. Like real-time interception of content data, real-time collection of traffic data is only effective if undertaken without the knowledge of the persons being investigated. Interception is surreptitious and must be carried out in such a manner that the communicating parties will not perceive the operation. Service providers and their employees knowing about the interception must, therefore, be

under an obligation of secrecy in order for the procedure to be undertaken effectively.

226. Paragraph 3 obligates Parties to adopt such legislative or other measures as may be necessary to oblige a service provider to keep confidential the fact of and any information about the execution of any of the measures provided in this article concerning the real-time collection of traffic data. This provision not only ensures the confidentiality of the investigation, but it also relieves the service provider of any contractual or other legal obligations to notify subscribers that data about them is being collected. Paragraph 3 may be effected by the creation of explicit obligations in the law. On the other hand, a Party may be able to ensure the confidentiality of the measure on the basis of other domestic legal provisions, such as the power to prosecute for obstruction of justice those persons who aid the criminals by telling them about the measure. Although a specific confidentiality requirement (with effective sanction in case of a breach) is a preferred procedure, the use of obstruction of justice offences can be an alternative means to prevent inappropriate disclosure and, therefore, also suffices to implement this paragraph. Where explicit obligations of confidentiality are created, these shall be subject to the conditions and safeguards as provided in Articles 14 and 15. These safeguards or conditions should impose reasonable time periods for the duration of the obligation, given the surreptitious nature of the investigative measure.

227. As noted above, the privacy interest is generally considered to be less with respect to the collection of

traffic data than interception of content data. Traffic data about time, duration and size of communication reveals little personal information about a person or his or her thoughts. However, a stronger privacy issue may exist in regard to data about the source or destination of a communication (e.g. the visited websites). The collection of this data may, in some situations, permit the compilation of a profile of a person's interests, associates and social context. Accordingly, Parties should bear such considerations in mind when establishing the appropriate safeguards and legal prerequisites for undertaking such measures, pursuant to Articles 14 and 15.

Interception of content data (Article 21)

228. Traditionally, the collection of content data in respect of telecommunications (e.g., telephone conversations) has been a useful investigative tool to determine that the communication is of an illegal nature (e.g., the communication constitutes a criminal threat or harassment, a criminal conspiracy or fraudulent misrepresentations) and to collect evidence of past or future crimes (e.g., drug trafficking, murder, economic crimes, etc.). Computer communications can constitute or afford evidence of the same types of criminality. However, given that computer technology is capable of transmitting vast quantities of data, including written text, visual images and sound, it has greater potential for committing crimes involving distribution of illegal content (e.g., child pornography). Many of the computer crimes involve the transmission or communication of data as part of their commission; for example, communications sent

to effect an illegal access of a computer system or the distribution of computer viruses. It is not possible to determine in real-time the harmful and illegal nature of these communications without intercepting the content of the message. Without the ability to determine and prevent the occurrence of criminality in progress, law enforcement would merely be left with investigating past and completed crimes where the damage has already occurred. Therefore, the real-time interception of content data of computer communications is just as, if not more, important as is the real-time interception of telecommunications.

229. 'Content data' refers to the communication content of the communication; i.e., the meaning or purport of the communication, or the message or information being conveyed by the communication. It is everything transmitted as part of the communication that is not traffic data.

230. Most of the elements of this article are identical to those of Article 20. Therefore, the comments, above, concerning the collection or recording of traffic data, obligations to co-operate and assist, and obligations of confidentiality apply equally to the interception of content data. Due to the higher privacy interest associated with content data, the investigative measure is restricted to 'a range of serious offences to be determined by domestic law'.

231. Also, as set forth in the comments above on Article 20, the conditions and safeguards applicable to real-time interception of content data may be more stringent than those applicable to the real-time collection of traffic data, or to the search and seizure or similar accessing or securing of stored data.

Section 3 - Jurisdiction

Jurisdiction (Article 22)

232. This Article establishes a series of criteria under which Contracting Parties are obliged to establish jurisdiction over the criminal offences enumerated in Articles 2-11 of the Convention.

233. Paragraph 1 littera a is based upon the principle of territoriality. Each Party is required to punish the commission of crimes established in this Convention that are committed in its territory. For example, a Party would assert territorial jurisdiction if both the person attacking a computer system and the victim system are located within its territory, and where the computer system attacked is within its territory, even if the attacker is not.

234. Consideration was given to including a provision requiring each Party to establish jurisdiction over offences involving satellites registered in its name. The drafters decided that such a provision was unnecessary since unlawful communications involving satellites will invariably originate from and/or be received on earth. As such, one of the bases for a Party's jurisdiction set forth in paragraph 1(a) – (c) will be available if the transmission originates or terminates in one of the locations specified therein. Further, to the extent the offence involving a satellite communication is committed by a Party's national outside the territorial jurisdiction of any State, there will be a jurisdictional basis under paragraph 1(d). Finally, the drafters questioned whether registration was an appropriate basis for

asserting criminal jurisdiction since in many cases there would be no meaningful nexus between the offence committed and the State of registry because a satellite serves as a mere conduit for a transmission.

235. Paragraph 1, litterae b and c are based upon a variant of the principle of territoriality. These litterae require each Party to establish criminal jurisdiction over offences committed upon ships flying its flag or aircraft registered under its laws. This obligation is already implemented as a general matter in the laws of many States, since such ships and aircraft are frequently considered to be an extension of the territory of the State. This type of jurisdiction is most useful where the ship or aircraft is not located in its territory at the time of the commission of the crime, as a result of which Paragraph 1, littera a would not be available as a basis to assert jurisdiction. If the crime is committed on a ship or aircraft that is beyond the territory of the flag Party, there may be no other State that would be able to exercise jurisdiction barring this requirement. In addition, if a crime is committed aboard a ship or aircraft which is merely passing through the waters or airspace of another State, the latter State may face significant practical impediments to the exercise of its jurisdiction, and it is therefore useful for the State of registry to also have jurisdiction.

236. Paragraph 1, littera d is based upon the principle of nationality. The nationality theory is most frequently applied by States applying the civil law tradition. It provides that nationals of a State are obliged to comply with the domestic law even when they are outside its territory. Under littera d, if a national commits an offence abroad, the Party is obliged to

have the ability to prosecute it if the conduct is also an offence under the law of the State in which it was committed or the conduct has taken place outside the territorial jurisdiction of any State.

237. Paragraph 2 allows Parties to enter a reservation to the jurisdiction grounds laid down in paragraph 1, litterae b, c, and d. However, no reservation is permitted with respect to the establishment of territorial jurisdiction under littera a, or with respect to the obligation to establish jurisdiction in cases falling under the principle of "aut dedere aut judicare" (extradite or prosecute) under paragraph 3, i.e. where that Party has refused to extradite the alleged offender on the basis of his nationality and the offender is present on its territory. Jurisdiction established on the basis of paragraph 3 is necessary to ensure that those Parties that refuse to extradite a national have the legal ability to undertake investigations and proceedings domestically instead, if sought by the Party that requested extradition pursuant to the requirements of "Extradition", Article 24, paragraph 6 of this Convention.

238. The bases of jurisdiction set forth in paragraph 1 are not the exclusive. Paragraph 4 of this Article permits the Parties to establish, in conformity with their domestic law, other types of criminal jurisdiction as well.

239. In the case of crimes committed by use of computer systems, there will be occasions in which more than one Party has jurisdiction over some or all of the participants in the crime. For example, many virus attacks, frauds and copyright violations committed through use of the Internet target victims located in

many States. In order to avoid duplication of effort, unnecessary inconvenience for witnesses, or competition among law enforcement officials of the States concerned, or to otherwise facilitate the efficiency or fairness of the proceedings, the affected Parties are to consult in order to determine the proper venue for prosecution. In some cases, it will be most effective for the States concerned to choose a single venue for prosecution; in others, it may be best for one State to prosecute some participants, while one or more other States pursue others. Either result is permitted under this paragraph. Finally, the obligation to consult is not absolute, but is to take place "where appropriate." Thus, for example, if one of the Parties knows that consultation is not necessary (e.g., it has received confirmation that the other Party is not planning to take action), or if a Party is of the view that consultation may impair its investigation or proceeding, it may delay or decline consultation.

Chapter III - International co-operation

240. Chapter III contains a number of provisions relating to extradition and mutual legal assistance among the Parties.

Section 1 - General principles

Title 1 – General principles relating to international co-operation

General principles relating to international co-

operation (Article 23)

241. Article 23 sets forth three general principles with respect to international co-operation under Chapter III.

242. Initially, the article makes clear that international co-operation is to be provided among Parties "to the widest extent possible." This principle requires Parties to provide extensive co-operation to each other, and to minimise impediments to the smooth and rapid flow of information and evidence internationally.

243. Second, the general scope of the obligation to co-operate is set forth in Article 23: co-operation is to be extended to all criminal offences related to computer systems and data (i.e. the offences covered by Article 14, paragraph 2, litterae a-b), as well as to the collection of evidence in electronic form of a criminal offence. This means that either where the crime is committed by use of a computer system, or where an ordinary crime not committed by use of a computer system (e.g., a murder) involves electronic evidence, the terms of Chapter III are applicable. However, it should be noted that Articles 24 (Extradition), 33 (Mutual assistance regarding the real time collection of traffic data) and 34 (Mutual assistance regarding the interception of content data) permit the Parties to provide for a different scope of application of these measures.

244. Finally, co-operation is to be carried out both "in accordance with the provisions of this Chapter" and "through application of relevant international agreements on international co-operation in criminal

matters, arrangements agreed to on the basis of uniform or reciprocal legislation, and domestic laws." The latter clause establishes the general principle that the provisions of Chapter III do not supersede the provisions of international agreements on mutual legal assistance and extradition, reciprocal arrangements as between the parties thereto (described in greater detail in the discussion of Article 27 below), or relevant provisions of domestic law pertaining to international co-operation. This basic principle is explicitly reinforced in Articles 24 (Extradition), 25 (General principles relating to mutual assistance), 26 (Spontaneous information), 27 (Procedures pertaining to mutual assistance requests in the absence of applicable international agreements), 28 (Confidentiality and limitation on use), 31 (Mutual assistance regarding accessing of stored computer data), 33 (Mutual assistance regarding the real-time collection of traffic data) and 34 (Mutual assistance regarding the interception of content data).

Title 2 – Principles relating to extradition

Extradition (Article 24)

245. Paragraph 1 specifies that the obligation to extradite applies only to offences established in accordance with Articles 2-11 of the Convention that are punishable under the laws of both Parties concerned by deprivation of liberty for a maximum period of at least one year or by a more severe penalty. The drafters decided to insert a threshold penalty because, under the Convention, Parties may punish some of the offences with a relatively short maximum

period of incarceration (e.g., Article 2 - illegal access - and Article 4 - data interference). Given this, the drafters did not believe it appropriate to require that each of the offences established in Articles 2-11 be considered per se extraditable. Accordingly, agreement was reached on a general requirement that an offence is to be considered extraditable if - as in Article 2 of the European Convention on Extradition (ETS N° 24) - the maximum punishment that could be imposed for the offence for which extradition was sought was at least one year's imprisonment. The determination of whether an offence is extraditable does not hinge on the actual penalty imposed in the particular case at hand, but instead on the maximum period that may legally be imposed for a violation of the offence for which extradition is sought.

246. At the same time, in accordance with the general principle that international co-operation under Chapter III should be carried out pursuant to instruments in force between the Parties, Paragraph 1 also provides that where a treaty on extradition or an arrangement on the basis of uniform or reciprocal legislation is in force between two or more Parties (see description of this term in discussion of Article 27 below) which provides for a different threshold for extradition, the threshold provided for in such treaty or arrangement shall apply. For example, many extradition treaties between European countries and non-European countries provide that an offence is extraditable only if the maximum punishment is greater than one year's imprisonment or there is a more severe penalty. In such cases, international extradition practitioners will continue to apply the normal threshold under their treaty practice in order

to determine whether an offence is extraditable. Even under the European Convention on Extradition (ETS N° 24), reservations may specify a different minimum penalty for extradition. Among Parties to that Convention, when extradition is sought from a Party that has entered such a reservation, the penalty provided for in the reservation shall be applied in determining whether the offence is extraditable.

247. Paragraph 2 provides that the offences described in paragraph 1 are to be deemed extraditable offences in any extradition treaty between or among the Parties, and are to be included in future treaties they may negotiate among themselves. This does not mean that extradition must be granted on every occasion on which a request is made but rather that the possibility of granting extradition of persons for such offences must be available. Under paragraph 5, Parties are able to provide for other requirements for extradition.

248. Under paragraph 3, a Party that would not grant extradition, either because it has no extradition treaty with the requesting Party or because the existing treaties would not cover a request made in respect of the offences established in accordance with this Convention, may use the Convention itself as a basis for surrendering the person requested, although it is not obligated to do so.

249. Where a Party, instead of relying on extradition treaties, utilises a general statutory scheme to carry out extradition, paragraph 4 requires it to include the offences described in Paragraph 1 among those for which extradition is available.

250. Paragraph 5 provides that the requested Party need not extradite if it is not satisfied that all of the terms and conditions provided for by the applicable treaty or law have been fulfilled. It is thus another example of the principle that co-operation shall be carried out pursuant to the terms of applicable international instruments in force between the Parties, reciprocal arrangements, or domestic law. For example, conditions and restrictions set forth in the European Convention on Extradition (ETS N° 24) and its Additional Protocols (ETS N°s 86 and 98) will apply to Parties to those agreements, and extradition may be refused on such bases (e.g., Article 3 of the European Convention on Extradition provides that extradition shall be refused if the offence is considered political in nature, or if the request is considered to have been made for the purpose of prosecuting or punishing a person on account of, inter alia, race, religion, nationality or political opinion).

251. Paragraph 6 applies the principle "aut dedere aut judicare" (extradite or prosecute). Since many States refuse extradition of their nationals, offenders who are found in the Party of which they are a national may avoid responsibility for a crime committed in another Party unless local authorities are obliged to take action. Under paragraph 6, if another Party has sought extradition of the offender, and extradition has been refused on the grounds that the offender is a national of the requested Party, the requested Party must, upon request of the requesting Party, submit the case to its authorities for the purpose of prosecution. If the Party whose extradition request has been refused does not request submission of the

case for local investigation and prosecution, there is no obligation on the requested Party to take action. Moreover, if no extradition request has been made, or if extradition has been denied on grounds other than nationality, this paragraph establishes no obligation on the requested Party to submit the case for domestic prosecution. In addition, paragraph 6 requires the local investigation and prosecution to be carried out with diligence; it must be treated as seriously "as in the case of any other offence of a comparable nature" in the Party submitting the case. That Party shall report the outcome of its investigation and proceedings to the Party that had made the request.

252. In order that each Party know to whom its requests for provisional arrest or extradition should be directed, paragraph 7 requires Parties to communicate to the Secretary General of the Council of Europe the name and address of its authorities responsible for making or receiving requests for extradition or provisional arrest in the absence of a treaty. This provision has been limited to situations in which there is no extradition treaty in force between the Parties concerned because if a bilateral or multilateral extradition treaty is in force between the Parties (such as ETS N° 24), the Parties will know to whom extradition and provisional arrest requests are to be directed without the necessity of a registration requirement. The communication to the Secretary General must be made at the time of signature or when depositing the Party's instrument of ratification, acceptance, approval or accession. It should be noted that designation of an authority does not exclude the possibility of using the diplomatic channel.

Title 3 – General principles relating to mutual assistance

General principles relating to mutual assistance (Article 25)

253. The general principles governing the obligation to provide mutual assistance are set forth in paragraph 1. Co-operation is to be provided "to the widest extent possible." Thus, as in Article 23 ("General principals relating to international co-operation"), mutual assistance is in principle to be extensive, and impediments thereto strictly limited. Second, as in Article 23, the obligation to co-operate applies in principle to both criminal offences related to computer systems and data (i.e. the offences covered by Article 14, paragraph 2, litterae a-b), and to the collection of evidence in electronic form of a criminal offence. It was agreed to impose an obligation to co-operate as to this broad class of crimes because there is the same need for streamlined mechanisms of international co-operation as to both of these categories. However, Articles 34 and 35 permit the Parties to provide for a different scope of application of these measures.

254. Other provisions of this Chapter will clarify that the obligation to provide mutual assistance is generally to be carried out pursuant to the terms of applicable mutual legal assistance treaties, laws and arrangements. Under paragraph 2, each Party is required to have a legal basis to carry out the specific forms of co-operation described in the remainder of the Chapter, if its treaties, laws and arrangements do not already contain such provisions. The availability

of such mechanisms, particularly those in Articles 29 through 35 (Specific provisions – Titles 1, 2, 3), is vital for effective co-operation in computer related criminal matters.

255. Some Parties will not require any implementing legislation in order to apply the provisions referred to in paragraph 2, since provisions of international treaties that establish detailed mutual assistance regimes are considered to be self-executing in nature. It is expected that Parties will either be able to treat these provisions as self executing, already have sufficient flexibility under existing mutual assistance legislation to carry out the mutual assistance measures established under this Chapter, or will be able to rapidly enact any legislation required to do so.

256. Computer data is highly volatile. By a few keystrokes or by operation of automatic programs, it may be deleted, rendering it impossible to trace a crime to its perpetrator or destroying critical proof of guilt. Some forms of computer data are stored for only short periods of time before being deleted. In other cases, significant harm to persons or property may take place if evidence is not gathered rapidly. In such urgent cases, not only the request, but the response as well should be made in an expedited manner. The objective of Paragraph 3 is therefore to facilitate acceleration of the process of obtaining mutual assistance so that critical information or evidence is not lost because it has been deleted before a request for assistance could be prepared, transmitted and responded to. Paragraph 3 does so by (1) empowering the Parties to make urgent requests for co-operation through expedited means of

communications, rather than through traditional, much slower transmission of written, sealed documents through diplomatic pouches or mail delivery systems; and (2) requiring the requested Party to use expedited means to respond to requests in such circumstances. Each Party is required to have the ability to apply this measure if its mutual assistance treaties, laws or arrangement do not already so provide. The listing of fax and e-mail is indicative in nature; any other expedited means of communication may be used as would be appropriate in the particular circumstances at hand. As technology advances, further expedited means of communicating will be developed that may be used to request mutual assistance. With respect to the authenticity and security requirement contained in the paragraph, the Parties may decide among themselves how to ensure the authenticity of the communications and whether there is a need for special security protections (including encryption) that may be necessary in a particularly sensitive case. Finally, the paragraph also permits the requested Party to require a formal confirmation sent through traditional channels to follow the expedited transmission, if it so chooses.

257. Paragraph 4 sets forth the principle that mutual assistance is subject to the terms of applicable mutual assistance treaties (MLATs) and domestic laws. These regimes provide safeguards for the rights of persons located in the requested Party that may become the subject of a request for mutual assistance. For example, an intrusive measure, such as search and seizure, is not executed on behalf of a requesting Party, unless the requested Party's fundamental

requirements for such measure applicable in a domestic case have been satisfied. Parties also may ensure protection of rights of persons in relation to the items seized and provided through mutual legal assistance.

258. However, paragraph 4 does not apply if "otherwise specifically provided in this Chapter." This clause is designed to signal that the Convention contains several significant exceptions to the general principle. The first such exception has been seen in paragraph 2 of this Article, which obliges each Party to provide for the forms of co-operation set forth in the remaining articles of the Chapter (such as preservation, real time collection of data, search and seizure, and maintenance of a 24/7 network), regardless of whether or not its MLATs, equivalent arrangements or mutual assistance laws currently provide for such measures. Another exception is found in Article 27 which is always to be applied to the execution of requests in lieu of the requested Party's domestic law governing international co-operation in the absence of an MLAT or equivalent arrangement between the requesting and requested Parties. Article 27 provides a system of conditions and grounds for refusal. Another exception, specifically provided for in this paragraph, is that co-operation may not be denied, at least as far as the offences established in Articles 2 – 11 of the Convention are concerned, on the grounds that the requested Party considers the request to involve a "fiscal" offence. Finally, Article 29 is an exception in that it provides that preservation may not be denied on dual criminality grounds, although the possibility of a reservation is provided for in this respect.

259. Paragraph 5 is essentially a definition of dual criminality for purposes of mutual assistance under this Chapter. Where the requested Party is permitted to require dual criminality as a condition to the providing of assistance (for example, where a requested Party has reserved its right to require dual criminality with respect to the preservation of data under Article 29, paragraph 4 "Expedited preservation of stored computer data"), dual criminality shall be deemed present if the conduct underlying the offence for which assistance is sought is also a criminal offence under the requested Party's laws, even if its laws place the offence within a different category of offence or use different terminology in denominating the offence. This provision was believed necessary in order to ensure that requested Parties do not adopt too rigid a test when applying dual criminality. Given differences in national legal systems, variations in terminology and categorisation of criminal conduct are bound to arise. If the conduct constitutes a criminal violation under both systems, such technical differences should not impede assistance. Rather, in matters in which the dual criminality standard is applicable, it should be applied in a flexible manner that will facilitate the granting of assistance.

Spontaneous information (Article 26)

260. This article is derived from provisions in earlier Council of Europe instruments, such as Article 10 of the Convention on the Laundering, Search, Seizure and Confiscation of the Proceeds from Crime (ETS N° 141) and Article 28 of the Criminal Law Convention

on Corruption (ETS N° 173). More and more frequently, a Party possesses valuable information that it believes may assist another Party in a criminal investigation or proceeding, and which the Party conducting the investigation or proceeding is not aware exists. In such cases, no request for mutual assistance will be forthcoming. Paragraph 1 empowers the State in possession of the information to forward it to the other State without a prior request. The provision was thought useful because, under the laws of some States, such a positive grant of legal authority is needed in order to provide assistance in the absence of a request. A Party is not obligated to spontaneously forward information to another Party; it may exercise its discretion in light of the circumstances of the case at hand. Moreover, the spontaneous disclosure of information does not preclude the disclosing Party, if it has jurisdiction, from investigating or instituting proceedings in relation to the facts disclosed.

261. Paragraph 2 addresses the fact that in some circumstances, a Party will only forward information spontaneously if sensitive information will be kept confidential or other conditions can be imposed on the use of information. In particular, confidentiality will be an important consideration in cases in which important interests of the providing State may be endangered should the information be made public, e.g., where there is a need to protect the identity of a means of collecting the information or the fact that a criminal group is being investigated. If advance inquiry reveals that the receiving Party cannot comply with a condition sought by the providing Party (for example, where it cannot comply with a

condition of confidentiality because the information is needed as evidence at a public trial), the receiving Party shall advise the providing Party, which then has the option of not providing the information. If the receiving Party agrees to the condition, however, it must honour it. It is foreseen that conditions imposed under this article would be consistent with those that could be imposed by the providing Party pursuant to a request for mutual assistance from the receiving Party.

Title 4 - Procedures pertaining to mutual assistance requests in the absence of applicable international agreements

Procedures pertaining to mutual assistance requests in the absence of applicable international agreements (Article 27)

262. Article 27 obliges the Parties to apply certain mutual assistance procedures and conditions where there is no mutual assistance treaty or arrangement on the basis of uniform or reciprocal legislation in force between the requesting and requested Parties. The Article thus reinforces the general principle that mutual assistance should be carried out through application of relevant treaties and similar arrangements for mutual assistance. The drafters rejected the creation of a separate general regime of mutual assistance in this Convention that would be applied in lieu of other applicable instruments and arrangements, agreeing instead that it would be more practical to rely on existing MLAT regimes as a general matter, thereby permitting mutual assistance practitioners to use the instruments and arrangements they are the most familiar with and

avoiding confusion that may result from the establishment of competing regimes. As previously stated, only with respect to mechanisms particularly necessary for rapid effective co-operation in computer related criminal matters, such as those in Articles 29-35 (Specific provisions – Title 1, 2, 3), is each Party required to establish a legal basis to enable the carrying out of such forms of co-operation if its current mutual assistance treaties, arrangements or laws do not already do so.

263. Accordingly, most forms of mutual assistance under this Chapter will continue to be carried out pursuant to the European Convention on Mutual Assistance in Criminal Matters (ETS N° 30) and its Protocol (ETS N° 99) among the Parties to those instruments. Alternatively, Parties to this Convention that have bilateral MLATs in force between them, or other multilateral agreements governing mutual assistance in criminal cases (such as between member States of the European Union), shall continue to apply their terms, supplemented by the computer- or computer-related crime-specific mechanisms described in the remainder of Chapter III, unless they agree to apply any or all of the provisions of this Article in lieu thereof. Mutual assistance may also be based on arrangements agreed on the basis of uniform or reciprocal legislation, such as the system of co-operation developed among the Nordic countries, which is also admitted by the European Convention on Mutual Assistance in Criminal Matters (Article 25, paragraph 4), and among members of the Commonwealth. Finally, the reference to mutual assistance treaties or arrangements on the basis of uniform or reciprocal legislation is not limited to

those instruments in force at the time of entry into force of the present Convention, but also covers instruments that may be adopted in the future.

264. Article 27 (Procedures pertaining to mutual assistance requests in the absence of applicable international agreements), paragraphs 2-10, provide a number of rules for providing mutual assistance in the absence of an MLAT or arrangement on the basis of uniform or reciprocal legislation, including establishment of central authorities, imposing of conditions, grounds for and procedures in cases of postponement or refusal, confidentiality of requests, and direct communications. With respect to such expressly covered issues, in the absence of a mutual assistance agreement or arrangement on the basis of uniform or reciprocal legislation, the provisions of this Article are to be applied in lieu of otherwise applicable domestic laws governing mutual assistance. At the same time, Article 27 does not provide rules for other issues typically dealt with in domestic legislation governing international mutual assistance. For example, there are no provisions dealing with the form and contents of requests, taking of witness testimony in the requested or requesting Parties, the providing of official or business records, transfer of witnesses in custody, or assistance in confiscation matters. With respect to such issues, Article 25, paragraph 4 provides that absent a specific provision in this Chapter, the law of the requested Party shall govern specific modalities of providing that type of assistance.

265. Paragraph 2 requires the establishment of a central authority or authorities responsible for sending and answering requests for assistance. The institution of

central authorities is a common feature of modern instruments dealing with mutual assistance in criminal matters, and it is particularly helpful in ensuring the kind of rapid reaction that is so useful in combating computer- or computer-related crime. Initially, direct transmission between such authorities is speedier and more efficient than transmission through diplomatic channels. In addition, the establishment of an active central authority serves an important function in ensuring that both incoming and outgoing requests are diligently pursued, that advice is provided to foreign law enforcement partners on how best to satisfy legal requirements in the requested Party, and that particularly urgent or sensitive requests are dealt with properly.

266. Parties are encouraged as a matter of efficiency to designate a single central authority for the purpose of mutual assistance; it would generally be most efficient for the authority designated for such purpose under a Party's MLATs, or domestic law to also serve as the central authority when this article is applicable. However, a Party has the flexibility to designate more than one central authority where this is appropriate under its system of mutual assistance. Where more than one central authority is established, the Party that has done so should ensure that each authority interprets the provisions of the Convention in the same way, and that both incoming and outgoing requests are treated rapidly and efficiently. Each Party is to advise the Secretary General of the Council of Europe of the names and addresses (including e-mail and fax numbers) of the authority or authorities designated to receive and respond to mutual assistance requests under this Article, and

Parties are obliged to ensure that the designation is kept up-to-date.

267. A major objective of a State requesting mutual assistance often is to ensure that its domestic laws governing the admissibility of evidence are fulfilled, and it can use the evidence before its courts as a result. To ensure that such evidentiary requirements can be met, paragraph 3 obliges the requested Party to execute requests in accordance with the procedures specified by the requesting Party, unless to do so would be incompatible with its law. It is emphasised that this paragraph relates only to the obligation to respect technical procedural requirements, not to fundamental procedural protections. Thus, for example, a requesting Party cannot require the requested Party to execute a search and seizure that would not meet the requested Party's fundamental legal requirements for this measure. In light of the limited nature of the obligation, it was agreed that the mere fact that the requested Party's legal system knows no such procedure is not a sufficient ground to refuse to apply the procedure requested by the requesting Party; instead, the procedure must be incompatible with the requested Party's legal principles. For example, under the law of the requesting Party, it may be a procedural requirement that a statement of a witness be given under oath. Even if the requested Party does not domestically have the requirement that statements be given under oath, it should honour the requesting Party's request.

268. Paragraph 4 provides for the possibility of refusing requests for mutual assistance requests brought under this Article. Assistance may be refused on the

grounds provided for in Article 25, paragraph 4 (i.e. grounds provided for in the law of the requested Party), including prejudice to the sovereignty of the State, security, ordre public or other essential interests, and where the offence is considered by the requested Party to be a political offence or an offence connected with a political offence. In order to promote the overriding principle of providing the widest measure of co-operation (see Articles 23, 25), grounds for refusal established by a requested Party should be narrow and exercised with restraint. They may not be so expansive as to create the potential for assistance to be categorically denied, or subjected to onerous conditions, with respect to broad categories of evidence or information.

269. In line with this approach, it was understood that apart from those grounds set out in Article 28, refusal of assistance on data protection grounds may be invoked only in exceptional cases. Such a situation could arise if, upon balancing the important interests involved in the particular case (on the one hand, public interests, including the sound administration of justice and, on the other hand, privacy interests), furnishing the specific data sought by the requesting Party would raise difficulties so fundamental as to be considered by the requested Party to fall within the essential interests ground of refusal. A broad, categorical, or systematic application of data protection principles to refuse cooperation is therefore precluded. Thus, the fact the Parties concerned have different systems of protecting the privacy of data (such as that the requesting Party does not have the equivalent of a specialised data protection authority) or have different means of

protecting personal data (such as that the requesting Party uses means other than the process of deletion to protect the privacy or the accuracy of the personal data received by law enforcement authorities), do not as such constitute grounds for refusal. Before invoking "essential interests" as a basis for refusing co-operation, the requested Party should instead attempt to place conditions which would allow the transfer of the data.

270. Paragraphs 5 permits the requested Party to postpone, rather than refuse, assistance where immediate action on the request would be prejudicial to investigations or proceedings in the requested Party. For example, where the requesting Party has sought to obtain evidence or witness testimony for purposes of investigation or trial, and the same evidence or witness are needed for use at a trial that is about to commence in the requested Party, the requested Party would be justified in postponing the providing of assistance.

271. Paragraph 6 provides that where the assistance sought would otherwise be refused or postponed, the requested Party may instead provide assistance subject to conditions. If the conditions are not agreeable to the requesting Party, the requested Party may modify them, or it may exercise its right to refuse or postpone assistance. Since the requested Party has an obligation to provide the widest possible measure of assistance, it was agreed that both grounds for refusal and conditions should be exercised with restraint.

272. Paragraph 7 obliges the requested Party to keep the requesting Party informed of the outcome of the

request, and requires reasons to be given in the case of refusal or postponement of assistance. The providing of reasons can, inter alia, assist the requesting Party to understand how the requested Party interprets the requirements of this Article, provide a basis for consultation in order to improve the future efficiency of mutual assistance, and provide to the requesting Party previously unknown factual information about the availability or condition of witnesses or evidence.

273. There are times when a Party makes a request in a particularly sensitive case, or in a case in which there could be disastrous consequences if the facts underlying the request were to be made public prematurely. Paragraph 8 accordingly permits the requesting Party to request that the fact and content of the request be kept confidential. Confidentiality may not be sought, however, to the extent that it would undermine the requested Party's ability to obtain the evidence or information sought, e.g., where the information will need to be disclosed in order to obtain a court order needed to effect assistance, or where private persons possessing evidence will need to be made aware of the request in order for it to be successfully executed. If the requested Party cannot comply with the request for confidentiality, it shall notify the requesting Party, which then has the option of withdrawing or modifying the request.

274. Central authorities designated in accordance with paragraph 2 shall communicate directly with one another. However, in case of urgency, requests for mutual legal assistance may be sent directly by judges and prosecutors of the requesting Party to the

judges and prosecutors of the requested Party. The judge or prosecutor following this procedure must also address a copy of the request made to his own central authority with a view to its transmission to the central authority of the requested Party. Under littera b, requests may be channelled through Interpol. Authorities of the requested Party that receive a request falling outside their field of competence, are, pursuant to littera c, under a two-fold obligation. First, they must transfer the request to the competent authority of the requested Party. Second, they must inform the authorities of the requesting Party of the transfer made. Under littera d, requests may also be transmitted directly without the intervention of central authorities even if there is no urgency, as long as the authority of the requested Party is able to comply with the request without making use of coercive action. Finally, littera e enables a Party to inform the others, through the Secretary General of the Council of Europe, that, for reasons of efficiency, direct communications are to be addressed to the central authority.

Confidentiality and limitation on use (Article 28)

275. This provision specifically provides for limitations on use of information or material, in order to enable the requested Party, in cases in which such information or material is particularly sensitive, to ensure that its use is limited to that for which assistance is granted, or to ensure that it is not disseminated beyond law enforcement officials of the requesting Party. These restrictions provide safeguards that are available for, inter alia, data protection purposes.

276. As in the case of Article 27, Article 28 only applies where there is no mutual assistance treaty, or arrangement on the basis of uniform or reciprocal legislation in force between the requesting and requested Parties. Where such treaty or arrangement is in force, its provisions on confidentiality and use limitations shall apply in lieu of the provisions of this Article, unless the Parties thereto agree otherwise. This avoids overlap with existing bilateral and multilateral mutual legal assistance treaties (MLATs) and similar arrangements, thereby enabling practitioners to continue to operate under the normal well-understood regime rather than seeking to apply two competing, possibly contradictory, instruments.

277. Paragraph 2 allows the requested Party, when responding to a request for mutual assistance, to impose two types of conditions. First, it may request that the information or material furnished be kept confidential where the request could not be complied with in the absence of such condition, such as where the identity of a confidential informant is involved. It is not appropriate to require absolute confidentiality in cases in which the requested Party is obligated to provide the requested assistance, as this would, in many cases, thwart the ability of the requesting Party to successfully investigate or prosecute crime, e.g. by using the evidence in a public trial (including compulsory disclosure).

278. Second, the requested Party may make furnishing of the information or material dependent on the condition that it not be used for investigations or proceedings other than those stated in the request. In order for this condition to apply, it must be expressly invoked by the requested Party, otherwise, there is

no such limitation on use by the requesting Party. In cases in which it is invoked, this condition will ensure that the information and material may only be used for the purposes foreseen in the request, thereby ruling out use of the material for other purposes without the consent of the requested Party. Two exceptions to the ability to limit use were recognised by the negotiators and are implicit in the terms of the paragraph. First, under fundamental legal principles of many States, if material furnished is evidence exculpatory to an accused person, it must be disclosed to the defence or a judicial authority. In addition, most material furnished under mutual assistance regimes is intended for use at trial, normally a public proceeding (including compulsory disclosure). Once such disclosure takes place, the material has essentially passed into the public domain. In these situations, it is not possible to ensure confidentiality to the investigation or proceeding for which mutual assistance was sought.

279. Paragraph 3 provides that if the Party to which the information is forwarded cannot comply with the condition imposed, it shall notify the providing Party, which then has the option of not providing the information. If the receiving Party agrees to the condition, however, it must honour it.

280. Paragraph 4 provides that the requesting Party may be required to explain the use made of the information or material it has received under conditions described in paragraph 2, in order that the requested Party may ascertain whether such condition has been complied with. It was agreed that the requested Party may not call for an overly

burdensome accounting e.g., of each time the material or information furnished was accessed.

Section 2 - Specific provisions

281. The aim of the present Section is to provide for specific mechanisms in order to take effective and concerted international action in cases involving computer-related offences and evidence in electronic form.

Title 1 - Mutual assistance regarding provisional measures

Expedited preservation of stored computer data (Article 29)

282. This article provides for a mechanism at the international level equivalent to that provided for in Article 16 for use at the domestic level. Paragraph 1 of this Article authorises a Party to make a request for, and paragraph 3 requires each Party to have the legal ability to obtain, the expeditious preservation of data stored in the territory of the requested Party by means of a computer system, in order that the data not be altered, removed or deleted during the period of time required to prepare, transmit and execute a request for mutual assistance to obtain the data. Preservation is a limited, provisional measure intended to take place much more rapidly than the execution of a traditional mutual assistance. As has been previously discussed, computer data is highly volatile. With a few keystrokes, or by operation of automatic programs, it may be deleted, altered or

moved, rendering it impossible to trace a crime to its perpetrator or destroying critical proof of guilt. Some forms of computer data are stored for only short periods of time before being deleted. Thus, it was agreed that a mechanism was required in order to ensure the availability of such data pending the lengthier and more involved process of executing a formal mutual assistance request, which may take weeks or months.

283. While much more rapid than ordinary mutual assistance practice, this measure is at the same time less intrusive. The mutual assistance officials of the requested Party are not required to obtain possession of the data from its custodian. The preferred procedure is for the requested Party to ensure that the custodian (frequently a service provider or other third party) preserve (i.e., not delete) the data pending the issuance of process requiring it to be turned over to law enforcement officials at a later stage. This procedure has the advantage of being both rapid and protective of the privacy of the person whom the data concerns, as it will not be disclosed to or examined by any government official until the criteria for full disclosure pursuant to normal mutual assistance regimes have been fulfilled. At the same time, a requested Party is permitted to use other procedures for ensuring the rapid preservation of data, including the expedited issuance and execution of a production order or search warrant for the data. The key requirement is to have an extremely rapid process in place to prevent the data from being irretrievably lost.

284. Paragraph 2 sets forth the contents of a request for preservation pursuant to this Article. Bearing in mind

that this is a provisional measure and that a request will need to be prepared and transmitted rapidly, the information provided will be summary and include only the minimum information required to enable preservation of the data. In addition to specifying the authority that is seeking preservation and the offence for which the measure is sought, the request must provide a summary of the facts, information sufficient to identify the data to be preserved and its location, and a showing that the data is relevant to the investigation or prosecution of the offence concerned and that preservation is necessary. Finally, the requesting Party must undertake to subsequently submit a request for mutual assistance so that it may obtain production of the data.

285. Paragraph 3 sets forth the principle that dual criminality shall not be required as a condition to providing preservation. In general, application of the principle of dual criminality is counterproductive in the context of preservation. First, as a matter of modern mutual assistance practice, there is a trend to eliminate the dual criminality requirement for all but the most intrusive procedural measures, such as search and seizure or interception. Preservation as foreseen by the drafters, however, is not particularly intrusive, since the custodian merely maintains possession of data lawfully in its possession, and the data is not disclosed to or examined by officials of the requested Party until after execution of a formal mutual assistance request seeking disclosure of the data. Second, as a practical matter, it often takes so long to provide the clarifications necessary to conclusively establish the existence of dual criminality that the data would be deleted, removed

or altered in the meantime. For example, at the early stages of an investigation, the requesting Party may be aware that there has been an intrusion into a computer in its territory, but may not until later have a good understanding of the nature and extent of damage. If the requested Party were to delay preserving traffic data that would trace the source of the intrusion pending conclusive establishment of dual criminality, the critical data would often be routinely deleted by service providers holding it for only hours or days after the transmission has been made. Even if thereafter the requesting Party were able to establish dual criminality, the crucial traffic data could not be recovered and the perpetrator of the crime would never be identified.

286. Accordingly, the general rule is that Parties must dispense with any dual criminality requirement for the purpose of preservation. However, a limited reservation is available under paragraph 4. If a Party requires dual criminality as a condition for responding to a request for mutual assistance for production of the data, and if it has reason to believe that, at the time of disclosure, dual criminality will not be satisfied, it may reserve the right to require dual criminality as a precondition to preservation. With respect to offences established in accordance with Articles 2 through 11, it is assumed that the condition of dual criminality is automatically met between the Parties, subject to any reservations they may have entered to these offences where permitted by the Convention. Therefore, Parties may impose this requirement only in relation to offences other than those defined in the Convention.

287. Otherwise, under paragraph 5, the requested Party may only refuse a request for preservation where its execution will prejudice its sovereignty, security, ordre public or other essential interests, or where it considers the offence to be a political offence or an offence connected with a political offence. Due to the centrality of this measure to the effective investigation and prosecution of computer- or computer-related crime, it was agreed that the assertion of any other basis for refusing a request for preservation is precluded.

288. At times, the requested Party will realise that the custodian of the data is likely to take action that will threaten the confidentiality of, or otherwise prejudice, the requesting Party's investigation (for example, where the data to be preserved is held by a service provider controlled by a criminal group, or by the target of the investigation himself).

In such situations, under paragraph 6, the requesting Party must be notified promptly, so that it may assess whether to take the risk posed by carrying through with the request for preservation, or to seek a more intrusive but safer form of mutual assistance, such as production or search and seizure.

289. Finally, paragraph 7 obliges each Party to ensure that data preserved pursuant to this Article will be held for at least 60 days pending receipt of a formal mutual assistance request seeking the disclosure of the data, and continue to be held following receipt of the request.

Expedited disclosure of preserved traffic data (Article 30)

290. This article provides the international equivalent of the power established for domestic use in Article 17. Frequently, at the request of a Party in which a crime was committed, a requested Party will preserve traffic data regarding a transmission that has travelled through its computers, in order to trace the transmission to its source and identify the perpetrator of the crime, or locate critical evidence. In doing so, the requested Party may discover that the traffic data found in its territory reveals that the transmission had been routed from a service provider in a third State, or from a provider in the requesting State itself. In such cases, the requested Party must expeditiously provide to the requesting Party a sufficient amount of the traffic data to enable identification of the service provider in, and path of the communication from, the other State. If the transmission came from a third State, this information will enable the requesting Party to make a request for preservation and expedited mutual assistance to that other State in order to trace the transmission to its ultimate source. If the transmission had looped back to the requesting Party, it will be able to obtain preservation and disclosure of further traffic data through domestic processes.

291. Under Paragraph 2, the requested Party may only refuse to disclose the traffic data, where disclosure is likely to prejudice its sovereignty, security, ordre public or other essential interests, or where it considers the offence to be a political offence or an offence connected with a political offence. As in

Article 29 (Expedited preservation of stored computer data), because this type of information is so crucial to identification of those who have committed crimes within the scope of this Convention or locating of critical evidence, grounds for refusal are to be strictly limited, and it was agreed that the assertion of any other basis for refusing assistance is precluded.

Title 2 - Mutual assistance regarding investigative powers

Mutual assistance regarding accessing of stored computer data (Article 31)

292. Each Party must have the ability to, for the benefit of another Party, search or similarly access, seize or similarly secure, and disclose data stored by means of a computer system located within its territory - just as under Article 19 (Search and seizure of stored computer data) it must have the ability to do so for domestic purposes. Paragraph 1 authorises a Party to request this type of mutual assistance, and paragraph 2 requires the requested Party to be able to provide it. Paragraph 2 also follows the applicable treaties, arrangements and domestic laws governing mutual legal assistance in criminal matters. Under paragraph 3, such a request must be responded to on an expedited basis where (1) there are grounds to believe that relevant data is particularly vulnerable to loss or modification, or (2) otherwise where such treaties, arrangements or laws so provide.

Transborder access to stored computer data with consent or where publicly available (Article 32)

293. The issue of when a Party is permitted to unilaterally

access computer data stored in another Party without seeking mutual assistance was a question that the drafters of the Convention discussed at length. There was detailed consideration of instances in which it may be acceptable for States to act unilaterally and those in which it may not. The drafters ultimately determined that it was not yet possible to prepare a comprehensive, legally binding regime regulating this area. In part, this was due to a lack of concrete experience with such situations to date; and, in part, this was due to an understanding that the proper solution often turned on the precise circumstances of the individual case, thereby making it difficult to formulate general rules. Ultimately, the drafters decided to only set forth in Article 32 of the Convention situations in which all agreed that unilateral action is permissible. They agreed not to regulate other situations until such time as further experience has been gathered and further discussions may be held in light thereof. In this regard, Article 39, paragraph 3 provides that other situations are neither authorised, nor precluded.

294. Article 32 (Trans-border access to stored computer data with consent or where publicly available) addresses two situations: first, where the data being accessed is publicly available, and second, where the Party has accessed or received data located outside of its territory through a computer system in its territory, and it has obtained the lawful and voluntary consent of the person who has lawful authority to disclose the data to the Party through that system. Who is a person that is "lawfully authorised" to disclose data may vary depending on the circumstances, the nature of the person and the

applicable law concerned. For example, a person's e-mail may be stored in another country by a service provider, or a person may intentionally store data in another country. These persons may retrieve the data and, provided that they have the lawful authority, they may voluntarily disclose the data to law enforcement officials or permit such officials to access the data, as provided in the Article.

Mutual assistance regarding the real-time collection of traffic data (Article 33)

295. In many cases, investigators cannot ensure that they are able to trace a communication to its source by following the trail through records of prior transmissions, as key traffic data may have been automatically deleted by a service provider in the chain of transmission before it could be preserved. It is therefore critical for investigators in each Party to have the ability to obtain traffic data in real time regarding communications passing through a computer system in other Parties. Accordingly, under Article 33 (Mutual assistance regarding the real-time collection of traffic data), each Party is under the obligation to collect traffic data in real time for another Party. While this Article requires the Parties to co-operate on these matters, here, as elsewhere, deference is given to existing modalities of mutual assistance. Thus, the terms and conditions by which such co-operation is to be provided are generally those set forth in applicable treaties, arrangements and laws governing mutual legal assistance in criminal matters.

296. In many countries, mutual assistance is provided broadly with respect to the real time collection of traffic data, because such collection is viewed as being less intrusive than either interception of content data, or search and seizure. However, a number of States take a narrower approach. Accordingly, in the same way as the Parties may enter a reservation under Article 14 (Scope of procedural provisions), paragraph 3, with respect to the scope of the equivalent domestic measure, paragraph 2 permits Parties to limit the scope of application of this measure to a more narrow range of offences than provided for in Article 23 (General principles relating to international co-operation). One caveat is provided: in no event may the range of offences be more narrow than the range of offences for which such measure is available in an equivalent domestic case. Indeed, because real time collection of traffic data is at times the only way of ascertaining the identity of the perpetrator of a crime, and because of the lesser intrusiveness of the measure, the use of the term "at least" in paragraph 2 is designed to encourage Parties to permit as broad assistance as possible, i.e., even in the absence of dual criminality.

Mutual assistance regarding the interception of content data (Article 34)

297. Because of the high degree of intrusiveness of interception, the obligation to provide mutual assistance for interception of content data is restricted. The assistance is to be provided to the extent permitted by the Parties' applicable treaties and laws. As the provision of co-operation for

interception of content is an emerging area of mutual assistance practice, it was decided to defer to existing mutual assistance regimes and domestic laws regarding the scope and limitation on the obligation to assist. In this regard, reference is made to the comments on Articles 14, 15 and 21 as well as to N° R (85) 10 concerning the practical application of the European Convention on Mutual Assistance in Criminal Matters in respect of letters rogatory for the interception of telecommunications.

Title 3 - 24/7 Network 24/7

Network (Article 35)

298. As has been previously discussed, effective combating of crimes committed by use of computer systems and effective collection of evidence in electronic form requires very rapid response. Moreover, with a few keystrokes, action may be taken in one part of the world that instantly has consequences many thousands of kilometres and many time zones away. For this reason, existing police co-operation and mutual assistance modalities require supplemental channels to address the challenges of the computer age effectively. The channel established in this Article is based upon the experience gained from an already functioning network created under the auspices of the G8 group of nations. Under this Article, each Party has the obligation to designate a point of contact available 24 hours per day, 7 days per week in order to ensure immediate assistance in investigations and proceedings within the scope of this Chapter, in particular as defined under Article 35, paragraph 1,

litterae a) – c). It was agreed that establishment of this network is among the most important means provided by this Convention of ensuring that Parties can respond effectively to the law enforcement challenges posed by computer- or computer-related crime.

299. Each Party's 24/7 point of contact is to either facilitate or directly carry out, inter alia, the providing of technical advice, preservation of data, collection of evidence, giving of legal information, and locating of suspects. The term "legal information" in Paragraph 1 means advice to another Party that is seeking co-operation of any legal prerequisites required for providing informal or formal co-operation.

300. Each Party is at liberty to determine where to locate the point of contact within its law enforcement structure. Some Parties may wish to house the 24/7 contact within its central authority for mutual assistance, some may believe that the best location is with a police unit specialised in fighting computer- or computer-related crime, yet other choices may be appropriate for a particular Party, given its governmental structure and legal system. Since the 24/7 contact is to provide both technical advice for stopping or tracing an attack, as well as such international co-operation duties as locating of suspects, there is no one correct answer, and it is anticipated that the structure of the network will evolve over time. In designating the national point of contact, due consideration should be given to the need to communicate with points of contacts using other languages.

301. Paragraph 2 provides that among the critical tasks to be carried out by the 24/7 contact is the ability to facilitate the rapid execution of those functions it does not carry out directly itself. For example, if a Party's 24/7 contact is part of a police unit, it must have the ability to co-ordinate expeditiously with other relevant components within its government, such as the central authority for international extradition or mutual assistance, in order that appropriate action may be taken at any hour of the day or night. Moreover, paragraph 2 requires each Party's 24/7 contact to have the capacity to carry out communications with other members of the network on an expedited basis.

302. Paragraph 3 requires each point of contact in the network to have proper equipment. Up-to-date telephone, fax and computer equipment will be essential to the smooth operation of the network, and other forms of communication and analytical equipment will need to be part of the system as technology advances. Paragraph 3 also requires that personnel participating as part of a Party's team for the network be properly trained regarding computer- or computer-related crime and how to respond to it effectively.

Chapter IV – Final provisions

303. With some exceptions, the provisions contained in this Chapter are, for the most part, based on the 'Model final clauses for conventions and agreements concluded within the Council of Europe' which were approved by the Committee of Ministers at the 315th

meeting of the Deputies in February 1980. As most of the articles 36 through 48 either use the standard language of the model clauses or are based on long-standing treaty-making practice at the Council of Europe, they do not call for specific comments. However, certain modifications of the standard model clauses or some new provisions require some explanation. It is noted in this context that the model clauses have been adopted as a non-binding set of provisions. As the Introduction to the Model Clauses pointed out "these model final clauses are only intended to facilitate the task of committees of experts and avoid textual divergences which would not have any real justification. The model is in no way binding and different clauses may be adapted to fit particular cases."

Signature and entry into force (Article 36)

304. Article 36, paragraph 1, has been drafted following several precedents established in other conventions elaborated within the framework of the Council of Europe, for instance, the Convention on the Transfer of Sentenced Persons and the Convention on Laundering, Search, Seizure and Confiscation of the Proceeds from Crime, which allow for signature, before their entry into force, not only by the member States of the Council of Europe, but also by non-member States which have participated in their elaboration. The provision is intended to enable the maximum number of interested States, not just members of the Council of Europe, to become Parties as soon as possible. Here, the provision is intended to apply to four non-member States, Canada, Japan,

South Africa and the United States of America, which actively participated in the elaboration of the Convention. Once the Convention enters into force, in accordance with paragraph 3, other non-member States not covered by this provision may be invited to accede to the Convention in conformity with Article 37, paragraph 1.

305. Article 36, paragraph 3 sets the number of ratifications, acceptances or approvals required for the Convention's entry into force at 5. This figure is higher than the usual threshold (3) in Council of Europe treaties and reflects the belief that a slightly larger group of States is needed to successfully begin addressing the challenge of international computer- or computer-related crime. The number is not so high, however, so as not to delay unnecessarily the Convention's entry into force. Among the five initial States, at least three must be Council of Europe members, but the two others could come from the four non-member States that participated in the Convention's elaboration. This provision would of course also allow for the Convention to enter into force based on expressions of consent to be bound by five Council of Europe member States.

Accession to the Convention (Article 37)

306. Article 37 has also been drafted on precedents established in other Council of Europe conventions, but with an additional express element. Under long-standing practice, the Committee of Ministers decides, on its own initiative or upon request, to invite a non-member State, which has not

participated in the elaboration of a convention, to accede to the convention after having consulted all contracting Parties, whether member States or not. This implies that if any contracting Party objects to the non-member State's accession, the Committee of Ministers would usually not invite it to join the convention. However, under the usual formulation, the Committee of Ministers could - in theory - invite such a non-member State to accede to a convention even if a non-member State Party objected to its accession. This means that - in theory - no right of veto is usually granted to non-member States Parties in the process of extending Council of Europe treaties to other non-member States. However, an express requirement that the Committee of Ministers consult with and obtain the unanimous consent of all Contracting States – not just members of the Council of Europe – before inviting a non-member State to accede to the Convention has been inserted. As indicated above, such a requirement is consistent with practice and recognises that all Contracting States to the Convention should be able to determine with which non-member States they are to enter into treaty relations. Nevertheless, the formal decision to invite a non-member State to accede will be taken, in accordance with usual practice, by the representatives of the contracting Parties entitled to sit on the Committee of Ministers. This decision requires the two-thirds majority provided for in Article 20.d of the Statute of the Council of Europe and the unanimous vote of the representatives of the contracting Parties entitled to sit on the Committee.

307. Federal States seeking to accede to the Convention, which intend to make a declaration under Article 41,

are required to submit in advance a draft of the statement referred to in Article 41, paragraph 3, so that the Parties will be in a position to evaluate how the application of the federal clause would affect the prospective Party's implementation of the Convention.(see paragraph 320).

Effects of the Convention (Article 39)

308. Article 39, paragraphs 1 and 2 address the Convention's relationship to other international agreements or arrangements. The subject of how conventions of the Council of Europe should relate to one another or to other treaties, bilateral or multilateral, concluded outside the Council of Europe is not dealt with by the Model Clauses referred to above. The usual approach utilised in Council of Europe conventions in the criminal law area (e.g., Agreement on Illicit Traffic by Sea (ETS N° 156)) is to provide that: (1) new conventions do not affect the rights and undertakings derived from existing international multilateral conventions concerning special matters; (2) Parties to a new convention may conclude bilateral or multilateral agreements with one another on the matters dealt with by the convention for the purposes of supplementing or strengthening its provisions or facilitating the application of the principles embodied in it; and (3) if two or more Parties to the new convention have already concluded an agreement or treaty in respect of a subject which is dealt with in the convention or otherwise have established their relations in respect of that subject, they shall be entitled to apply that agreement or treaty or to regulate those relations

accordingly, in lieu of the new convention, provided this facilitates international co-operation.

309. Inasmuch as the Convention generally is intended to supplement and not supplant multilateral and bilateral agreements and arrangements between Parties, the drafters did not believe that a possibly limiting reference to "special matters" was particularly instructive and were concerned that it could lead to unnecessary confusion. Instead, paragraph 1 of Article 39 simply indicates that the present Convention supplements other applicable treaties or arrangements as between Parties and it mentions in particular three Council of Europe treaties as non-exhaustive examples: the 1957 European Convention on Extradition (ETS N° 24), the 1959 European Convention on Criminal Matters (ETS N° 30) and its 1978 Additional Protocol (ETS N° 99). Therefore, regarding general matters, such agreements or arrangements should in principle be applied by the Parties to the Convention on cybercrime. Regarding specific matters only dealt with by this Convention, the rule of interpretation lex specialis derogat legi generali provides that the Parties should give precedence to the rules contained in the Convention. An example is Article 30, which provides for the expedited disclosure of preserved traffic data when necessary to identify the path of a specified communication. In this specific area, the Convention, as lex specialis, should provide a rule of first resort over provisions in more general mutual assistance agreements.

310. Similarly, the drafters considered language making the application of existing or future agreements contingent on whether they "strengthen" or

"facilitate" co-operation as possibly problematic, because, under the approach established in the international co-operation Chapter, the presumption is that Parties will apply relevant international agreements and arrangements.

311. Where there is an existing mutual assistance treaty or arrangement as a basis for co-operation, the present Convention would only supplement, where necessary, the existing rules. For example, this Convention would provide for the transmission of mutual assistance requests by expedited means of communications if such a possibility does not exist under the original treaty or arrangement.

312. Consistent with the Convention's supplementary nature and, in particular, its approach to international co-operation, paragraph 2 provides that Parties are also free to apply agreements that already are or that may in the future come into force. Precedent for such an articulation is found in the Transfer of Sentenced Persons Convention (ETS N° 112). Certainly, in the context of international co-operation, it is expected that application of other international agreements (many of which offer proven, longstanding formulas for international assistance) will in fact promote co-operation. Consistent with the terms of the present Convention, Parties may also agree to apply its international co-operation provisions in lieu of such other agreements). In such instances the relevant co-operation provisions set forth in Article 27 would supersede the relevant rules in such other agreements. As the present Convention generally provides for minimum obligations, Article 39, paragraph 2 recognises that Parties are free to assume obligations that are more specific in addition to those

already set out in the Convention, when establishing their relations concerning matters dealt with therein. However, this is not an absolute right: Parties must respect the objectives and principles of the Convention when so doing and therefore cannot accept obligations that would defeat its purpose.

313. Further, in determining the Convention's relationship to other international agreements, the drafters also concurred that Parties may look for additional guidance to relevant provisions in the Vienna Convention on the Law of Treaties.

314. While the Convention provides a much-needed level of harmonisation, it does not purport to address all outstanding issues relating to computer- or computer-related crime. Therefore, paragraph 3 was inserted to make plain that the Convention only affects what it addresses. Left unaffected are other rights, restrictions, obligations and responsibilities that may exist but that are not dealt with by the Convention. Precedent for such a "savings clause" may be found in other international agreements (e.g., UN Terrorist Financing Convention).

Declarations (Article 40)

315. Article 40 refers to certain articles, mostly in respect of the offences established by the Convention in the substantive law section, where Parties are permitted to include certain specified additional elements which modify the scope of the provisions. Such additional elements aim at accommodating certain conceptual or legal differences, which in a treaty of global ambition are more justified than they perhaps

might be in a purely Council of Europe context. Declarations are considered acceptable interpretations of Convention provisions and should be distinguished from reservations, which permit a Party to exclude or to modify the legal effect of certain obligations set forth in the Convention. Since it is important for Parties to the Convention to know which, if any, additional elements have been attached by other Parties, there is an obligation to declare them to the Secretary General of the Council of Europe at the time of signature or when depositing an instrument of ratification, acceptance, approval or accession. Such notification is particularly important concerning the definition of offences, as the condition of dual criminality will have to be met by the Parties when applying certain procedural powers. No numerical limit was felt necessary in respect of declarations.

Federal clause (Article 41)

316. Consistent with the goal of enabling the largest possible number of States to become Parties, Article 41 allows for a reservation which is intended to accommodate the difficulties federal States may face as a result of their characteristic distribution of power between central and regional authorities. Precedents exist outside the criminal law area for federal declarations or reservations to other international agreements (11). Here, Article 41 recognises that minor variations in coverage may occur as a result of well-established domestic law and practice of a Party which is a federal State. Such variations must be based on its Constitution or other fundamental

principles concerning the division of powers in criminal justice matters between the central government and the constituent States or territorial entities of a federal State. There was agreement among the drafters of the Convention that the operation of the federal clause would only lead to minor variations in the application of the Convention.

317. For example, in the United States, under its Constitution and fundamental principles of federalism, federal criminal legislation generally regulates conduct based on its effects on interstate or foreign commerce, while matters of minimal or purely local concern are traditionally regulated by the constituent States. This approach to federalism still provides for broad coverage of illegal conduct encompassed by this Convention under US federal criminal law, but recognises that the constituent States would continue to regulate conduct that has only minor impact or is purely local in character. In some instances, within that narrow category of conduct regulated by State but not federal law, a constituent State may not provide for a measure that would otherwise fall within the scope of this Convention. For example, an attack on a stand-alone personal computer, or network of computers linked together in a single building, may only be criminal if provided for under the law of the State in which the attack took place; however the attack would be a federal offence if access to the computer took place through the Internet, since the use of the Internet provides the effect on interstate or foreign commerce necessary to invoke federal law. The implementation of this Convention through United States federal law,

or through the law of another federal State under similar circumstances, would be in conformity with the requirements of Article 41.

318. The scope of application of the federal clause has been restricted to the provisions of Chapter II (substantive criminal law, procedural law and jurisdiction). Federal States making use of this provision would still be under the obligation to co-operate with the other Parties under Chapter III, even where the constituent State or other similar territorial entity in which a fugitive or evidence is located does not criminalise conduct or does not have procedures required under the Convention.

319. In addition, paragraph 2 of Article 41 provides that a federal State, when making a reservation under paragraph 1 of this Article, may not apply the terms of such reservation to exclude or substantially diminish its obligations to provide for measures set forth in Chapter II. Overall, it shall provide for a broad and effective law enforcement capability with respect to those measures. In respect of provisions the implementation of which come within the legislative jurisdiction of the constituent States or other similar territorial entities, the federal government shall refer the provisions to the authorities of these entities with a favourable endorsement, encouraging them to take appropriate action to give them effect. .

Reservations (Article 42)

320. Article 42 provides for a number of reservation possibilities. This approach stems from the fact that

the Convention covers an area of criminal law and criminal procedural law which is relatively new to many States. In addition, the global nature of the Convention, which will be open to member and non-member States of the Council of Europe, makes having such reservation possibilities necessary. These reservation possibilities aim at enabling the largest number of States to become Parties to the Convention, while permitting such States to maintain certain approaches and concepts consistent with their domestic law. At the same time, the drafters endeavoured to restrict the possibilities for making reservations in order to secure to the largest possible extent the uniform application of the Convention by the Parties. Thus, no other reservations may be made than those enumerated. In addition, reservations may only be made by a Party at the time of signature or upon deposit of its instrument of ratification, acceptance, approval or accession.

321. Recognising that for some Parties certain reservations were essential to avoid conflict with their constitutional or fundamental legal principles, Article 43 imposes no specific time limit for the withdrawal of reservations. Instead, they should be withdrawn as soon as circumstances so permit.

322. In order to maintain some pressure on the Parties and to make them at least consider withdrawing their reservations, the Convention authorises the Secretary General of the Council of Europe to periodically enquire about the prospects for withdrawal. This possibility of enquiry is current practice under several Council of Europe instruments. The Parties are thus given an opportunity to indicate whether they still need to maintain their reservations in

respect of certain provisions and to withdraw, subsequently, those which no longer prove necessary. It is hoped that over time Parties will be able to remove as many of their reservations as possible so as promote the Convention's uniform implementation.

Amendments (Article 44)

323. Article 44 takes its precedent from the Convention on Laundering, Search, Seizure and Confiscation of the Proceeds from Crime (ETS N° 141), where it was introduced as an innovation in respect of criminal law conventions elaborated within the framework of the Council of Europe. The amendment procedure is mostly thought to be for relatively minor changes of a procedural and technical character. The drafters considered that major changes to the Convention could be made in the form of additional protocols.

324. The Parties themselves can examine the need for amendments or protocols under the consultation procedure provided for in Article 46. The European Committee on Crime Problems (CDPC) will in this regard be kept periodically informed and required to take the necessary measures to assist the Parties in their efforts to amend or supplement the Convention.

325. In accordance with paragraph 5, any amendment adopted would come into force only when all Parties have informed the Secretary General of their acceptance. This requirement seeks to ensure that the Convention will evolve in a uniform manner.

Settlement of disputes (Article 45)

326. Article 45, paragraph 1, provides that the European Committee on Crime Problems (CDPC) should be kept informed about the interpretation and application of the provisions of the Convention. Paragraph 2 imposes an obligation on the Parties to seek a peaceful settlement of any dispute concerning the interpretation or the application of the Convention. Any procedure for solving disputes should be agreed upon by the Parties concerned. Three possible mechanisms for dispute-resolution are suggested by this provision: the European Committee on Crime Problems (CDPC) itself, an arbitral tribunal or the International Court of Justice.

Consultations of the Parties (Article 46)

327. Article 46 creates a framework for the Parties to consult regarding implementation of the Convention, the effect of significant legal, policy or technological developments pertaining to the subject of computer- or computer-related crime and the collection of evidence in electronic form, and the possibility of supplementing or amending the Convention. The consultations shall in particular examine issues that have arisen in the use and implementation of the Convention, including the effects of declarations and reservations made under Articles 40 and 42.

328. The procedure is flexible and it is left to the Parties to decide how and when to convene if they so wish. Such a procedure was believed necessary by the drafters of the Convention to ensure that all Parties to the Convention, including non-member States of

the Council of Europe, could be involved - on an equal footing basis - in any follow-up mechanism, while preserving the competences of the European Committee on Crime Problems (CDPC). The latter shall not only be kept regularly informed of the consultations taking place among the Parties, but also facilitate those and take the necessary measures to assist the Parties in their efforts to supplement or amend the Convention. Given the needs of effective prevention and prosecution of cyber-crime and the associated privacy issues, the potential impact on business activities, and other relevant factors, the views of interested parties, including law enforcement, non-governmental and private sector organisations, may be useful to these consultations.

329. Paragraph 3 provides for a review of the Convention's operation after 3 years of its entry into force, at which time appropriate amendments may be recommended. The CDPC shall conduct such review with the assistance of the Parties.

330. Paragraph 4 indicates that except where assumed by the Council of Europe it will be for the Parties themselves to finance any consultations carried out in accordance with paragraph 1 of Article 46. However, apart from the European Committee on Crime Problems (CDPC), the Council of Europe Secretariat shall assist the Parties in their efforts under the Convention.

Bibliography

Computer-Based National Information Systems: Technology and Public Policy Issues Office of Technology Assessment, US Congress, Washington, DC, 1981.

Culnan, M. J., "The Dimensions of Perceived Accessibility to Information: Implications for the Delivery of Information Systems and Services", *Journal of the American Society for Information Science* 36, no. 5, 1985:302-305.

Daniel, Evelyn, 'Information resources and organisational structure', *Journal of the American Society for Information Science*, 1983.

Davis Dwight B., "Supercomputers: A Strategic Imperative?" *High Technology*, May 1984.

Davis Ruth M., "Computers and Electronics for Individual Services", *Science*, February 12, 1982.

Jonsher, C. (1983). "Information Resources and Economic Productivity", *Information Economics and Policy*, vol. 1, no. 1.

Lynch, Clifford and Preston, Cecelia M. 'Internet access to information resources', *Annual Review of Information Science and Technology*, 25, 1990.

Lynn, M.S., 'Digital Preservation and Access', *Collection Management* 22, nos. 3/4/1998.

Maciuszko, Kathleen, 'A quiet revolution: community online system', *Online*, Nov. 1990, 24-32.

Hebrawi, B. *Open systems interconnection: upper layer standards and practices*, London, McGraw-Hill, 1992.

Hayes J. E. and D. Michie (eds), *Intelligent Systems: The Unprecedented Opportunity* Ellis Horwood, Chichester, England, 1983.

Horowitz Irving Louis, "Printed Words, Computers and Democratic Societies", *The Virginia Quarterly Review*, Autumn 1983.

Galliers, R. 'Information systems and technology planning within a competitive strategy framework', in *Information Management. State of the Art Report*, P. Griffiths (ed.), Pergamon, 1986.

Garland Roy, *Microcomputers and Children in the Primary School* Falmer Press, London, 1982.

Halevi G., *The Role of Computers in Manufacturing Processes*, John Wiley, New York, 1982.

Hawkridge David, *New Information Technology in Education*, Croom Helm, London, 1983.

Kahin, Brian, *Building information infrastructure: issue in the development of the National Research and Education Network*, London, McGraw-Hill, 1992.

Kim, W. H. (1980), "Challenge to US Domination: The Promise of Technology for Newly Industrialised Countries", in *Financial Times Conference: World Electronic Strategies for Success* London.

Maciuszko, Kathleen, 'A quiet revolution: community online system', *Online*, Nov. 1990, 24-32.

Nash Deanna C. and David A. Bollier, "Protecting Privacy in the Age of Hometech", *Technology Review*, August-September 1981.

Parsons, G. L. 'Information technology: a new competitive weapon', *Sloan Management Review*, Autumn 1983.

Smith, Christine H. (ed.), *Open Systems Interconnection: the Communications Technology of the 1990s*, London, KG Saur, 1988.

Whisler, Thomas, *The Impact of Computer on Organisation*, Praeger, 1970.

Index